109

Punk Record Labels and the Struggle for Autonomy

Critical Media Studies

Series Editor
Andrew Calabrese, University of Colorado

This series covers a broad range of critical research and theory about media in the modern world. It includes work about the changing structures of the media, focusing particularly on work about the political and economic forces and social relations which shape and are shaped by media institutions, structural changes in policy formation and enforcement, technological transformations in the means of communication, and the relationships of all these to public and private cultures worldwide. Historical research about the media and intellectual histories pertaining to media research and theory are particularly welcome. Emphasizing the role of social and political theory for informing and shaping research about communications media, Critical Media Studies addresses the politics of media institutions at national, subnational, and transnational levels. The series is also interested in short, synthetic texts on key thinkers and concepts in critical media studies.

Titles in the series

Punk Record Labels and the Struggle for Autonomy

The Emergence of DIY

Alan O'Connor

LEXINGTON BOOKS

A division of
ROWMAN & LITTLEFIELD PUBLISHERS, INC.
Lanham • Boulder • New York • Toronto • Plymouth, UK

LEXINGTON BOOKS

A division of Rowman & Littlefield Publishers, Inc.
A wholly owned subsidiary of The Rowman & Littlefield Publishing Group, Inc.
4501 Forbes Boulevard, Suite 200
Lanham, MD 20706

Estover Road
Plymouth PL6 7PY
United Kingdom

British Library Cataloguing in Publication Information Available

Library of Congress Cataloging-in-Publication Data
O'Connor, Alan.
    Punk record labels and the struggle for autonomy : the emergence of DIY / Alan
O'Connor.
      p. cm. — (Critical media studies)
    Includes bibliographical references (p.   ) and index.
    ISBN-13: 978-0-7391-2659-2 (cloth : alk. paper)
    ISBN-10: 0-7391-2659-8 (cloth : alk. paper)
    ISBN-13: 978-0-7391-2660-8 (pbk. : alk. paper)
    ISBN-10: 0-7391-2660-1 (pbk. : alk. paper)
    1. Punk rock music—Marketing. 2. Sound recording industry. I. Title.
ML3790.O33 2008
306.4'8426—dc22   2008004143

Printed in the United States of America

⊗™ The paper used in this publication meets the minimum requirements of
American National Standard for Information Sciences—Permanence of Paper
for Printed Library Materials, ANSI/NISO Z39.48-1992.

"I'm feeling rejected; I'm feeling left out." —Gray Matter

"I'm miles behind on the road to success." —Floodgate

Contents

Introduction

This book is about punk record labels and the struggle to be autonomous. These record labels are mostly unknown outside the punk-rock scene. Some, like Dischord and Alternative Tentacles, have operated for more than twenty-five years. Others are just starting out. A few labels such as Profane Existence and Havoc Records are anarchist but most simply describe themselves as independent. The variety of music runs from harsh grindcore to melodic pop punk. Different labels tend to specialize in a certain sound and the range of music inevitably reflects the tastes of the person doing the label. Many of these record labels are run by one or two people, but some have between five and twenty employees. The people who do them come from different backgrounds but most are middle-class kids. Many of these are dropouts from the middle class. All of this affects struggles for autonomy.

To be autonomous means that you make your own decisions. The classic sociologist Max Weber says that in autonomous organizations "the order governing the organization has been established by its own members on their own authority."[1] The opposite of this is when order has been imposed from outside the organization. It is quite difficult for a record label to be completely autonomous. Many people have to register with the state that they are "doing business as" the name of their label. At some point the record label will have to face the decision whether to incorporate and pay business taxes. When the label has employees there are regulations about payroll taxes and insurance. If a record label signs contracts with bands these are legal documents which may result in lawsuits. As well as this, in the 1980s there were some famous cases where punk record labels and distributors were prosecuted for obscenity.[2]

But when we speak of the autonomy of punk record labels we usually mean in relation to major labels. In 1977 the major record labels controlled about 90 percent of the music industry in the United States. Today the four major labels account for 87.4 percent of physical and digital album sales.[3] It is true that the punk explosions of the 1970s and the 1990s supported many independent record labels and expanded indie record distribution. But the majors were sometimes interested in signing punk bands too. They hoped that bands like Hüsker Dü and Green Day would be successful. In the United States a record goes gold when it sells 500,000 copies.[4] But as the music industry diversified over the past twenty years, the major labels were sometimes interested in a band like Sonic Youth that might not have an instant hit but steady sales within a specialized market. As well as this, in the 1990s each major label bought or established their own indie distribution business. It is almost impossible today to get into large chain stores and big-box retailers without going through a distribution subsidiary of the major labels. This system also allows the majors to keep an eye on fast-breaking bands that they might want to sign themselves.

Among the bigger punk labels, Epitaph gets into the system through ADA. Fat Wreck and Victory Records go through RED. Dischord gets in because their distributor Southern Records has a deal with Fontana (and before that with Caroline). The Black Flag record label SST has had a difficult time over the years with its distributors. In November 2001 their distributor DNA went bankrupt and they are now with Koch, a large corporation that distributes video games, DVDs and CDs. Koch also signs bands that have been dropped by major labels and markets them to college radio. The other members of the Dead Kennedys won a lawsuit against Jello Biafra and Alternative Tentacles for not properly exploiting the band's back catalog. Those records are now issued by Manifesto, which is distributed by Navarre, another large corporation like Koch and also not owned by a major label.[5]

Table 0.1. Major Record Labels in the United States

Major Label	Indie Distributor
EMI	Caroline
Sony BMG	RED
Universal Music Group	Fontana
Warner Music Group	ADA

Kate: About 70 percent of Bouncing Souls titles on Epitaph sell in chain stores. 30 percent in independent stores. But I think that is an Epitaph trend. Of the Chunksaah titles maybe half and half. It's hard to get in those stores. You have to do huge buy-ins. A lot of time you have to agree to some marketing thing. That's when I get kinda indignant. Who are you? You want me to pay you to carry my records? (Interview no. 28, with Chunksaah)[6]

The alternative to the music industry is to do it yourself. Each generation of punks discovers that it is not difficult to record songs and have them pressed. At this underground level today the recordings are mostly sold by the band at its shows, traded with other small labels and distributed to indie record stores. In this DIY scene records might sell between 1,000 and 3,000 copies. With recording costs for a 7" at $500 and for an album between $3,000 and $7,000 (many bands can do it cheaper) the break-even point comes as low as 2,000 copies sold. Getting to 10,000 is punk-rock gold, though this is increasingly difficult because there has been a general decline of sales of DIY punk records in the past five years.[7]

This book is based on interviews with sixty-one records labels, mainly in the United States but including four in Spain and four from Canada. They all consider themselves to be independent punk labels but the field is quite diverse. Some operate from a kid's bedroom and others have an office or small warehouse. Record distributors are also part of the story because one of the biggest problems facing a record label is getting the music into stores. Mention must also be made of punk fanzines that review releases, carry advertisements and in some cases play a crucial role in shaping the culture and ideals of the punk scene. The real-estate market and the cost of renting space in different cities also come into the story. But this book is centrally about small punk record labels and the people who run them.

In the mid-1980s I read punk fanzines like *Maximumrocknroll* and bought records by the Dicks and the Dead Kennedys. A few years later I lived in a punk house in Toronto and got to experience the underground straightedge scene. I started to do a distribution of anarchist, queer and riot grrrl records and zines at punk shows. Kids would look through my boxes and say something like: "You have different records than everyone else." This eventually turned into Who's Emma which was a volunteer-run record store and infoshop that started in Toronto in 1996. At Who's Emma we had huge debates about the meaning of punk and whether we should sell records on major labels or distributed by major labels. We had fights about bands that were anti-abortion and about record covers that some people thought were sexist. Selling records at cheap prices and supporting underground bands were always important, but beyond that it was hard to get agreement on anything. This book tries to take the debate further.

I'd like to thank everyone who I interviewed at record labels. Also Martin Sprouse who talked to me about *Maximumrocknroll* during the life of his close friend Tim Yohannan. Thanks to people who read the manuscript, especially Allan Antliff and Stephe Perry. Warren Kovoch helped with statistics and prepared the diagrams in chapter Four.

Notes

1. Max Weber, *Economy and Society*, quoted in Jeremy F. Lane, *Pierre Bourdieu: A Critical Introduction* (London: Pluto Press, 2000), 183.

2. For legal problems related to the Dead Kennedys's album *Frankenchrist* see David Kennedy, "Frankenchrist versus the State: The New Right, Rock Music and the Case of Jello Biafra," *Journal of Popular Culture* 24, no. 1 (1990): 131–48. Also Ruth Schwartz, "This IS Art! Jello is Free!" *Maximumrocknroll* no. 53, October 1987, 5 pages. Available online at www.operationphoenixrecords.com (30 April 2007). For similar problems in Canada, Rob Bowman, "Argh Fuck Kill–Canadian Hardcore Goes on Trial: The Case of the Dayglo Abortions," in *Policing Pop*, ed. Martin Cloonan and Reebee Garofalo (Philadelphia: Temple University Press, 2003), 113–39. The problems of Flux of Pink Indians and Crass are described by Martin Cloonan, "I Fought the Law: Popular Music and British Obscenity Law," *Popular Music* 14, no. 3 (1995): 349–63.

3. In the late 1970s the major labels in the USA were CBS, RCA, WEA, MCA, Polygram and Capitol. Simon Frith, *Sound Effects: Youth, Leisure and the Politics of Rock'n'Roll* (London: Constable, 1983), 138. For today's figures see, "2006 U.S. Music Purchases Exceed 1 Billion Sales," online at http://homebusinesswire.com (12 February 2007). The situation is not quite so bad in Canada, where indie labels have 17.24 percent of album sales in 2006. "10 percent Growth in Overall Music Sales," online at http://homebusinesswire.com (9 February 2007).

4. An album also goes gold when it sells 40,000 copies in Spain, 50,000 in Canada, or 100,000 in the UK. The figure is set relative to each country's population.

5. For Jello Biafra's side of the story see the interview in V. Vale ed. *Real Conversations: Henry Rollins, Jello Biafra, Lawrence Ferlinghetti, Billy Childish* (San Francisco: RE/search, 2001), 167–70. And for the other side www.deadkennedysnews (7 June 2007). The band recently issued a statement saying that the Dead Kennedys's back catalog in total is now selling 130,000 copies a year. Navarre also handles distribution for Revelation to chain record stores. Koch previously distributed labels such as Epitaph, Hopeless, Gearhead, Artimus and Go-Kart Records.

6. Complete details about all interviews for this book can be found in Appendix B.

7. At Dischord Records the maximum recording budget for an album is usually $3,000. (Interview no. 61, with Dischord Records.)

CHAPTER ONE

The Struggle for Autonomy

Punks argue endlessly about record labels. After all, if the Ramones were on a major label what is the problem? How can you get more punk than the Ramones? The simple answer is that punk has a history that goes back more than thirty years. It is a mistake to regard punk as a *thing* and then to argue about its true spirit or meaning. Punk is an activity or a series of activities that take place in time. This has changed quite dramatically over three decades. Most modern punks don't look a bit like the Ramones in their tight jeans, skinny T-shirts, and leather jackets. And most punk bands from the 1980s and 1990s don't sound very much like the Ramones. Impatient writers in the letters column of *Maximumrocknroll* fanzine might argue that the Ramones were punk and on a major label and so what's the problem? But the more experienced columnists understand that the punk scene changes over time. They've been around and seen the changes.

The Ramones were actually signed to Sire Records, founded by Seymour Stein in 1966. Much of its business involved licensing European acts like Fleetwood Mac for release in the United States. By the early 1970s the label was looking to release its own bands. The Ramones signed with Sire in late 1975 because no big record label would even listen to them. Although it was an independent label, Stein operated no differently from the majors. The band signed a contract and got an advance of about $6,000 to record their first album and $20,000 for band expenses. Stein also forced the band to allow his company to handle their publishing rights.[1] Sire later signed a distribution deal with Warner Bros. Records and the first Ramones album to benefit from

1

major-label distribution was Rocket to Russia.[2] About 1978 Sire was acquired by or formed a partnership with Warner. The major label then wanted to make the Ramones more suitable for radio play.[3]

The UK Subs are a first-generation English punk group. The band started in London in 1977. The Subs contributed a couple of songs to a punk compilation album, recorded a session for John Peel's Radio One show and released their first single on City Records in 1978. On the basis of this success the band was signed to GEM Records, a subsidiary of the major label RCA. Back then punk singles could reach the Top Forty and the UK Subs soon found themselves performing on the "Top of the Pops" television program. Guitarist Nicky Garratt eventually moved to the United States, working for a time as a consultant for independent record distribution. His own New Red Archives record label has the rights to some of the UK Subs material. But much to his frustration, he has not been able to get back the early recordings from other labels.[4]

All the old punk bands were not on major labels. Many first-generation bands issued their records themselves or were on small labels. Today these records are rare collectors' items or reissued on Killed By Death compilations of obscure early punk bands. Some of these bands undoubtedly hoped to gain the attention of a major label. Others were probably just caught up in the fun of releasing their own record. Apart from a small number of famous bands in England most of the early punks existed on the margins of the record industry. Those involved with the mainstream were often on subsidiaries of major labels, or small labels with relationships with the majors. The vast majority of punk bands in the late 1970s and early 1980s never even got that far. For them, doing it yourself was not a choice but a necessity. The music industry was mostly not interested.

This first generation of punk was quite diverse. It included semi-professional musicians who had played in bands before 1977, people on the fringes of the art world, and young kids who were just inspired by seeing punk on television. Some of these bands had professional management and others were completely clueless. Some of them wanted to challenge the music industry, some wanted careers as musicians and others were just in it for the fun. With this kind of diversity there was a wide range of ways of doing things. For a few brief years it seemed that almost anything was possible. Bands were experimenting with all kinds of strategies.

In the early days Black Flag and the Dead Kennedys attempted to release records on labels that were distributed by a major.[5] In both cases the reason was to get better distribution. Black Flag's *Damaged* LP from November 1981 was originally to be co-released by the band's own label SST and Unicorn, which had a distribution deal with MCA. The major label refused to handle it because of an unrelated financial dispute with Unicorn. The first pressing has the MCA logo covered by a sticker. The second pressing has the Unicorn logo on the back. Unicorn and SST were then engaged in a legal battle and for a while Black Flag was not allowed to issue any records. Unicorn went bankrupt in late 1983. The *Damaged* album was later reissued on SST Records.[6] The band MDC was also considering a contract with Unicorn in 1982, but in the end decided against it.[7]

The Dead Kennedys attempted something similar when they signed in 1980 to Miles Axe Copeland's I.R.S Records. The attraction was that I.R.S. had a distribution deal with A&M Records. In the 1970s A&M was the third largest label in the United States in terms of album sales. Although technically an independent for most of the decade, A&M signed a manufacturing and distribution deal with RCA in February 1979, firmly bringing it into the orbit of the major label. In fact, the Dead Kennedys deal with I.R.S. didn't go through because A&M objected to the band's name and still embarrassed by its brush with the Sex Pistols in England, exercised its right to not promote and distribute the Dead Kennedys's album. Copeland then released *Fresh Fruit For Rotting Vegetables* on his Faulty Products label. An online history of I.R.S. Records hints that A&M was actually involved in distributing the Dead Kennedys's record for the first few months. *Fresh Fruit For Rotting Vegetables* was later reissued on Alternative Tentacles.[8] It is only looking back that we say that Black Flag and the Dead Kennedys couldn't possibly have been flirting with labels that had links to majors. Didn't they have their own record labels?

But also at this time popular punk bands could sell surprisingly well by today's standards. Successful bands were attempting to get wide distribution into the record stores. The first pressing of Black Flag's *Damaged* LP was 20,000 copies. At its peak, the band apparently sold about 60,000 copies. The Dead Kennedy's *Fresh Fruit For Rotting Vegetables* sold over 70,000 copies in the United Kingdom alone. Exact figures are hard to come by, but it seems that by the mid-1980s the Dead Kennedys's records had sold about 150,000 copies each.[9] All of this changed by the early to mid-1980s. Joe Carducci reports that a popular touring band backed by a business-like record label and good distribution into indie record stores (that's what he worked at) could not achieve sales of 40,000 copies.[10] Punk rock had changed and gone underground.

Nobody talks about the punk "community" without putting that word in quotes. It is simply too spread out and there is so much diversity that the idea of a face-to-face community is unconvincing. Perhaps there is a community

in your hometown. The most usual term used is the punk scene. Some people dislike that term because it seems trendy and superficial but the word has
gained in meaning as it is used. The punk scene includes bands, record labels,
distributors, some indie record stores, punk zines, show promoters and places
to play. It can even include cheap places to eat and local places when punks
hang out. Everyone knows that there are regional differences (these were especially important in the 1980s), there are many different kinds of punk music and that punks argue endlessly about politics.

The French sociologist and anti-globalization activist Pierre Bourdieu has
a term for this. What punks call a scene he calls a cultural field. It is a useful
idea. In his book *The Rules of Art* he discusses the field of modern literature
in France. The book also deals with theater, poetry and Bourdieu elsewhere
writes about Manet's painting. Bourdieu's book starts with the French novelist Gustave Flaubert, whose famous modern novel *Sentimental Education* was
published in 1869. Most writers about art discuss it in terms of brilliant or tal-
ented individuals. Bourdieu is different because he concentrates on the social
conditions that make their work possible. It is difficult to be a novelist if
there are no publishers or bookstores and part of what Bourdieu is showing is
the emergence of a middle-class market to support novelists and artists. But
there is also a heroic moment when writers and painters reject that market.
Just as Bourdieu wrote about the genesis of the field of modern art, it is possible to show the emergence of the field of American hardcore punk by the
early 1980s.[11]

A field is a relatively autonomous space in society where a specialized activity takes place. Medicine, law, genetic research, literature and art are all
fields. In turn they exist within the field of power (the state regulates the
practice of medicine) and the economic field (big business is very interested
in genetic research). A field exists when a struggle has taken place for its autonomy, though this cannot be taken for granted and always has to be
guarded. One of the major issues in every field is its boundaries (where does
medicine end and nursing begin). Bourdieu always argues for the autonomy
of fields because he thinks they work best when people are judged by their
peers and rewarded on that basis. A field works best when it is autonomous
and not subject to direct interference by the state or by economic forces.
When Ian MacKaye says that punk is a "free space" he is expressing a similar idea. The general argument of this book is that punk in 1977 was wide
open to economic pressures but that by the early 1980s punk had become a
more or less autonomous field.

There are a couple of reasons why the field was formed at this time. The
first is that the major-label recording industry lost interest in punk. As far as

they were concerned it was all over. Most of them were relieved and returned to marketing rock music that they understood. They knew how to deal with Bruce Springsteen but the Sex Pistols and their friends had been a nightmare. The second reason is that the sound of hardcore bands is relatively unmarketable. When a younger generation of bands in the early 1980s decided to play fast thrash music they removed themselves from the field of commercial rock music. For some of them this may have been a conscious decision, but for many young bands it simply resulted from the desire to compete with other underground bands and to play faster. They just didn't care. The third essential condition was that there emerged a means of communication within the hardcore scene. Fanzines had always been important in punk. But *Maximumrocknroll* was different. It was published by people who were older than hardcore kids and who had well-defined political principles. *Maximumrocknroll* would hold people responsible for their actions. Of course it would always be controversial, but this collective oversight is an essential condition for the emergence of an autonomous field.

In the confused mix of the first wave of punk there were some tendencies that were quite anti-commercial. These often involved people from an arts rather than a music business background. Early punk record labels in the United States like Bomp!, Posh Boy, Slash and Frontier were all run by music industry people or cultural entrepreneurs (Greg Shaw, Robbie Fields, Bob Biggs, Lisa Fancher). These labels often faded out after the initial wave of punk bands or diversified into other forms of music. Dangerhouse Records in Los Angeles was quite different. It was operated on a small scale by Dave Brown and others associated with the Screamers. There was actually a group of people that lived together in the Danger House, perhaps similar to Dischord House in the Washington, DC area.[12]

Dischord Records was started by members of the Teen Idles band in Washington DC. The band broke up and the members decided to release their songs on a 7" record. Ian MacKaye was impressed by the Dangerhouse records and by the fact that they were documenting punk bands in their own city.

Table 1.1.   Early Punk Record Labels in the USA

Record Label	Year	Founders	Bands on Label
Bomp!	1974	Greg Shaw	Modern Lovers, Dead Boys
Dangerhouse	1977	Dave Brown, Pat Garrett, Black Randy	Weirdos, Avengers, The Dils
Posh Boy	1978	Robbie Fields	Social Distortion, Agent Orange
Slash	1978	Bob Biggs	Germs, X, Fear
Frontier	1979	Lisa Fancher	Circle Jerks, Adolescents, T.S.O.L.

Although not an obsessive record collector he had carefully bought all the Dangerhouse releases and liked their consistency and creative packaging. The members of the Teen Idles were not only very young, they had no connection whatsoever with the music industry. As Ian says:

> We didn't have a business model at all, frankly, because we didn't know how to do it. A guy here in town—Skip Groff, who ran a record store called Yesterday And Today—he had a label called Limp and he gave us the phone number for the place where records were made. He said, "Just send them the money and they'll make you the records."[13]

Far from the music industry in Los Angeles, the members of the Teen Idles invented their own way of doing things. The sleeves for the first six records were folded and glued by hand. Although they didn't know it at the time, Dischord Records was setting the standard for the field of hardcore punk labels. Quite a number of DIY labels today mention Dischord as an example of how to do it. One person remarked that people today have been influenced by Dischord even if they don't realize it. Its low prices and no-nonsense approach to issuing records helped shape the DIY hardcore scene that emerged in the United States.

Maximumrocknroll started as a radio show in 1977. Tim Yohannan managed "through the back door" to get a program on KPFA in Berkeley, part of the Pacifica chain of community radio stations. It had a powerful signal and the punk rock show reached most of North California each week. The program lasted until about 1990 when KPFA cancelled it because Pacifica was trying to reach more upscale listener-supporters. At that point *Maximumrocknroll* did the weekly show on cassette and 20 to 30 radio stations subscribed to the service for $5 a week.[14] Yohannan explains:

> MRR is not just a radio program. The aim of the show is to be the on-the-air outlet for what's happening here and for people to be able to use the show as a vehicle for their communications. Radio and TV should be something that is part of a community. It should not be something separate that's run by some company. I've tried to get MRR to not only be supportive of the continuing underground of music, but because we have a historical perspective in terms of what happened in the '50s and '60s with outbursts of cultural rebellion, and how that was co-opted or destroyed, that definitely shapes our attitude towards what's going on now. We try and play the real gut level stuff in whatever musical form it takes, the stuff that is definitely still in rebellion. But we don't just play records, we also take an advocacy position—how do we get the local scene to grow and perpetuate, and not get ripped off or co-opted.[15]

Five years after the radio show began, *Maximumrocknroll* started publication as a magazine. From 1982 to the present it appears monthly (at first it appeared every two months), printed on cheap newsprint paper and without a glossy cover. Its initial printing of 3,000 copies expanded to 10,000 by 1984 and about 15,000 in the mid-1990s.[16] Although *Flipside* magazine shared some of the same ground and much of the same values, *Maximumrocknroll* shaped the field of hardcore punk in the early 1980s. It did this by combining intelligent articles and reviews, leftist politics and support for a non-commercial hardcore punk scene.[17] It had a lively letters section in each issue. The idea of printing scene reports was brilliant and established the idea that each city and region should have a punk scene. There was a strong international focus from the beginning with special reports from Brazil, Finland and other countries. *Maximumrocknroll* gave space to bands that had something to say and the idea quickly developed that hardcore bands ought to have more or less articulate political opinions.

By issue number five the zine was well established. That issue carried display advertisements for eighteen record labels (including one from Finland). These were all independents. In the 1980s many punk records were sold by mail order. A review or an ad in *Maximumrocknroll* was the most important conduit for reaching punk record buyers, not only in the United States but throughout the world. Punks from that time tell stories of getting their monthly copy of the zine and circling the records they wanted to order. Letters were sent off with U.S. dollar bills carefully concealed in the envelope. People who released records in the 1980s tell stories of how a single ad or review in MRR could result in 300 or 400 orders through the mail. This is quite significant because by this time many of these records were pressed in editions of 1,000 copies.

Yohannan was by all accounts a charismatic person. He seems to have been well aware of the power that *Maximumrocknroll* soon exerted on the scene as a whole. In a way this made him uncomfortable but he was also unabashed about his own leftist political views. Described by his close friend Martin Sprouse as "too anarchist to be a good socialist" he had no problem describing himself as a Marxist. This was not a position shared by all contributors to MRR and so a diversity of views appeared in the zine, especially among the regular columnists. (There was also a rule that forbade columnists from criticizing each other in print that Yohannan would occasionally use to block criticism in the magazine about his decisions, on the grounds that he was also a regular columnist.) Needless to say, much of the American punk scene in the 1980s did not share Yohannan's socialist politics. There was soon a blood feud between the zine and East Coast straightedge bands. But because MRR was so well-organized and appeared like clockwork each month it had a huge influence on shaping the practices and values of DIY punk. Its nonprofit operation allowed the zine to be independent of the music industry. It was never far from controversy.[18]

> Ryan: In my early days I was Tim Yo is right on. His words are gold. I love the fact that he was such an asshole. If you don't follow my guidelines of what is punk I'm not going to put you in my magazine. (Interview no. 17, with Punks Before Profits)

> Ian: It seems to me that in the late 80s and early 90s punk was blowing up and this created a challenge for Tim and MRR. They were out of space for ads, so to make room they started tightening their criteria for what they considered "punk," and then rejecting those ads that didn't meet their definition. I don't remember Dischord being rejected, but it's entirely possible. I do know that Tim and I quarreled quite a bit about the subject. Tim had an orthodox take on punk rock and we knocked heads from time to time because I totally disagreed with him about this. I didn't and still don't agree that punk is merely a sound or a style. I think of punk rock as a free space. I thought it was short-sighted on behalf of MRR to draw such a hard line, but considering they are still in business it's only fair to consider their approach as successful. (Interview no. 61, with Dischord Records)

Crass Records in England was another influence on the emerging hardcore punk scene. Although few record labels in the United States from the 1990s mention it as a direct influence, it helped shape the field in much the same way as Dischord Records did in the United States. Crass was a band that operated as a collective and even lived together in a farmhouse in Essex. The band started in 1977 in the mould of the Sex Pistols or Sham 69 but was different in that it took anarchist politics seriously. It was in many ways a continuation of the anti-authoritarian culture of the 1960s. Crass quickly developed into releasing its own records, with distinctive fold-out posters and a low retail price boldly printed on the cover. Pay No More Than. . . . This in turn developed into several related record labels that soon sponsored a new generation of anarcho-punk bands. The influence of this movement was to be seen in a release by Conflict, Only Stupid Bastards Help EMI (New Army Records, 1986). "There is no reason for this LP to cost more than 2.99 pounds—if you are asked for more: DON'T BUY IT." Boycott E.M.I. It was the influence of Crass that made this seem perfectly reasonable for hardcore punks by 1986. The anarcho-punk movement happened mainly in Britain and Europe but also included bands in the USA such as Crucifix, Heart Attack and White Cross.[19]

Felix Havoc: My number one influence was Dischord. Still probably the best U.S. punk label, along with Dangerhouse. Other big inspirations were Crass and Mortarhate and also Pusmort. The Havoc Label is a rip of the Pusmort logo (I just copied Pushead's lettering off the *Cleanse the Bacteria* comp). At the time Tribal War, Ebullition and Profane Existence as well as Sound Pollution were labels I aspired to be like, and later Prank really set the standard for quality that I tried to emulate when I started doing LPs and CDs as well as 7"s. I read everything I could find in old MRRs about different labels and Dischord was really the template I tried to follow, low prices, fair dealings with the bands, and dealing direct with small stores and distributors. (Interview no. 12, with Havoc Records)

Nate: It came from *Maximumrocknroll*. I didn't get all my ethics from them but a small brainwashing. Definitely Dischord. Those two guys are very on top of their shit. The fact that they have so much integrity. If you want it you buy it. When they were approached by majors they weren't interested. Crass not so much. I have Crass records. They probably influenced things that influenced me. Like Dropdead. More indirectly. (Interview no. 22, with Gloom Records)

The final factor in the emergence of hardcore punk as a field by the early 1980s is the music itself. For many people, of course, this is the most important matter. There was a huge diversity of punk sounds in 1977. By the early 1980s most of these bands had faded away. Hardcore music was fast, aggressive, and from a commercial point of view virtually unmarketable. At this point everything begins to converge. The indie labels that had jumped onto the punk wave were generally not interested in hardcore. (Frontier Records was started because Bomp! had no interest in the new hardcore bands.) Often the bands themselves had to release their own records. X-Claim Records in Boston was basically a name used by SS Decontrol and their friends to put out their own records in 1982 and 1983. It became the norm for bands to release their own records or for it to be done by a friend. *Maximumrocknroll* championed this punk or hardcore sound. A compilation of punk and hardcore bands was issued in co-operation with the Jello Biafra's Alternative Tentacles record label. *Not So Quiet on the Western Front* defined the range of sounds and the state of the game in hardcore punk as it emerged into the early 1980s.[20]

Notes

1. Jim Bessman, *Ramones: An American Band* (New York: St. Martin's Press, 1993), 41–43.

2. Bessman, *Ramones*, 90–91. Sire was working in co-operation with major labels. A double 7" compilation *New Wave Rock'n'roll: Get behind it before it gets past you* was issued as a promo for retailers by Sire and EMI (Australia) in 1977.

3. Bessman, *Ramones*, 118.

4. Ian Glasper, *Burning Britain: The Story of UK Punk 1980–1984* (London: Cherry Red Books, 2004), 246. See also interview by Allan McNaughton, "UK Subs," *Maximumrocknroll* no. 168, May 1997, 6 pages. Gem Records went bankrupt in 1981 and the UK Subs switched to NEMS, an independent label.

5. In the late 1970s the major labels in the USA were CBS, RCA, WEA, MCA, Polygram and Capitol. Together they accounted for 90 percent of the market. Simon Frith, *Sound Effects: Youth, Leisure and the Politics of Rock'n'Roll* (London: Constable, 1983), 138. An underground label like Subterranean in San Francisco signed contracts with bands in the beginning but then gave this up and worked with bands on trust. (Interview no. 47, with Subterranean)

6. Michael Azerrad, *Our Band Could Be Your Life: Scenes from the American Indie Underground 1981–1991* (Boston: Little, Brown and Company, 2001), 36–37. David Grad, "Black Flag: An Oral History," in *We Owe You Nothing: Punk Planet: The Collected Interviews*, ed. Daniel Sinker (New York: Akashic Books, 2001), 77–93. See also Joe Carducci, *Rock and the Pop Narcotic* (Chicago: Redoubt Press, 1990), 112–13. Carducci was manager at SST from 1981–1986. For Black Flag's discography see Burkdard Jaerisch, *FLEX! U.S. Hardcore Discography*, 2d ed. (Germany: Flex, 2001).

7. "Flipside Interviews Millions of Dead Cops (MDC)," *Flipside* no. 36, 1982, online at www.operationphoenixrecords.com (17 February 2007).

8. It also seems that the Dead Kennedys, continuing some of the Sex Pistols's pranks on the music industry, wanted to release *Fresh Fruit for Rotting Vegetables* on December 25. But it was apparently released in November in time for the Christmas rush of record sales. For the history of I.R.S. records see www.irscorner.com (14 February 2007). The clearest account of the relationship between Faulty / I.R.S. and the Dead Kennedys is George Hurchalla, *Going Underground: American Punk 1979–1992* (Stuart, FL: Zuo Press, 2006), 15–16. For A&M sales figures see Geoffrey P. Hull, *The Recording Industry*, second edition (New York: Routledge, 2004), 124. A&M Records released two albums by the Dickies in 1979.

9. Michael W. Dean, e-mail to author, 9 February 2007. Dean was given this figure by East Bay Ray in 1985. In a discussion published in *Maximumrocknroll* no. 9 in 1984, Biafra said in response to a direct question from Tim Yohannan that: "Basically we have been able to live for the past 3 years on income from the band. So on a day-to-day subsistence and existence level we've risen to *that level*, which is a lot further than many other people in the punk scene have been able to do, and that breeds a certain amount of jealousy. I take great pride in the fact that we've been able to support ourselves through the band without working 8 hours a day at degrading shit jobs that tax our energy and creativity." Online at Kill From the Heart website http://homepages.nyu.edu/~cch223/usa/info/mrr_discussion.html (17 April 2007). Sales figures for *Fresh Fruit For Rotting Vegetables* in the UK are from a press clipping re-

produced in f-Stop Fitzgerald, *Dead Kennedys: The Unauthorized Version* (San Francisco: Last Gasp, 1983), 42. At the time of the *Frankenchrist* album trial it was mentioned that the pressing was 30,000 copies. See Suzanne Stefanac, "DK's AT, Mordam Bust," *Maximumrocknroll* no. 36, July 1986, 1 page. It is widely reported that the Dead Kennedys's back catalog sells in total about 100,000 copies each year. (A figure of 80,000 is sometimes mentioned.) The most popular albums must have sold more than 350,000 copies each.

10. Carducci, *Rock and the Pop Narcotic*, 54.

11. Pierre Bourdieu, *The Rules of Art: Genesis and Structure of the Literary Field*, trans. Susan Emanuel (Stanford: Stanford University Press, 1996). The discussion of Manet is in Pierre Bourdieu, *The Field of Cultural Production* (New York: Columbia University Press, 1993).

12. Ian MacKaye mentions Danger House and compares it to Dischord House in Interview no. 61. Greg Shaw worked for United Artists, was a band manager, a music journalist for *Creem* and other magazines, and publisher of *Who Put the Bomp!* There is a good interview about Poshboy at www.spontaneous.com (17 April 2007) and Robbie Fields memoirs are online at www.geocities.com/posh-boy (30 June 2006). Slash Records was associated with the Los Angeles fanzine of the same name, but the record label signed a distribution deal with Warner around 1981 and Bob Biggs has worked in the music industry since then. Lisa Fancher worked at Bomp! and started Frontier Records because Greg Shaw was not interested in hardcore punk bands. She previously wrote for fanzines and *Sounds* magazine. See interview at www.spontaneous.com (30 June 2006). The Dangerhouse label mainly released 7" records of Los Angeles bands from 1977–1979. For a memoir about the label by Dave Brown and an interview see Generic, "Pioneers of Punk: Dangerhouse," *Maximumrocknroll* 179, April 1998, 4 pages. There is also a Web page dedicated to Dangerhouse that draws on an interview done by Tim Yohannan in *Maximumrocknroll* #99 at www.breakmyface.com (28 June 2006).

13. Matthew Fritch, online interview with Ian MacKaye at www.magnetmagazine.com (29 June 2006).

14. Scott M. X. Turner, "Maximizing Rock and Roll: An Interview with Tim Yohannan," in *Sounding Off! Music as Subversion / Resistance / Revolution*, ed. Ron Sakolsky and Fred Wei-Han-Ho (New York: Autonomedia, 1995), 180–94. There is an amount of punk folklore about conflicts between Dischord Records and *Maximumrocknroll*. It is therefore worth noting that Ian Mackaye and Tim Yohannan got along very well. "We were dear friends. . . ." Ian says in Interview no. 61. Martin Sprouse says in an interview with the author that "Ian and Tim had been friends forever." In the 1990s Fugazi would stay at the *Maximumrocknroll* house when they were on tour. Although they had different musical tastes the two friends could stay up all night talking.

15. "Interview with Maximum Rock N' Roll: More than Just a Radio Show," *Ripper* no. 5, 1981. Online at http://homepages.nyu.edu/~cch223/usa/info/mrr_ripperinter .html (16 April 2007).

16. Circulation figures from Jeff Goldthorpe, "Interview with Maximum Rock and Roll," *Radical America* 18, no. 6 (1984): 10; and Turner, "Maximizing Rock and Roll" (1995), 181. About 1,000 copies of the magazine were sold in Europe and for a while in the mid 1980s there were hopes of printing a European edition. There is an editorial note about this in *Maximumrocknroll* no, 36, May 1986, 1 page.

17. A decade later *Flipside* took a somewhat different approach to major labels than MRR. It accepted their ads but at twice the rate that indies were charged. It defined indie as independent of major label distribution, accounting and billing. See *Flipside* no. 85, July–August 1993, 1 page.

18. A policy was decided upon in the mid-1990s to concentrate on music related to the garage, punk and hardcore that *Maximumrocknroll* was founded to cover. "Releases that don't fit that focus don't get regular reviews and can only be in ads which feature other reviewable releases. These bands can be reviewed in the genre specific columns, but they don't get interviews." Column by Tom Hopkins, *Maximumrocknroll* no. 178, March 1998, 2 pages. Hopkins was responsible for listening to about 200 records each month and distributing them to the 40 music reviewers. He personally reviewed emo bands such as Antioch Arrow and Shotmaker in his own column. *Maximumrocknroll* previously refused to accept ads for Equal Vision Records because of the record label's Krishna identity. Mordam Records declined for the same reason to distribute Equal Vision. (Interview with Martin Sprouse about MRR, interview with an ex-employee of Mordam Records, and interview no. 21, with Equal Vision Records.) The zine also has a history of challenging nationalist sentiments within the punk scene. After September 11, 2001 it was involved in a dispute with TKO Records because the new coordinators refused to accept an ad that featured a large stylized American flag. See letters in *Maximumrocknroll* no. 225, February 2002, 2 pages.

Heartattack zine was started in 1994 during the major label punk explosion. It was dedicated to the underground hardcore scene and had even tighter economic criteria for ads and music reviews than MRR. *Heartattack* would not accept anything with UPC codes, with any connection to a major label (including press and distribution deals) or even financed by the larger indies such as Dutch East, Caroline, Cargo and Helter Skelter. The immediate motive for starting the new zine was MRR's refusal to review a double LP by the band Still Life because of its musical style. Kent McClard wanted to challenge Yohannan's influence on the punk scene and to champion underground emo, straightedge and different forms of hardcore music. See editorial statement in *Heartattack* no. 1, March 1994, 2 pages. Some issues of *Heartattack* (but not this one) are available online at www.operationphoenixrecords.com (7 May 2007). The zine ceased publishing in 2006. *Punk Planet* started in 1994 and also ceased publishing, in 2007 after 80 issues. It was more professional than *Heartattack* but not as closely linked to the underground hardcore scene.

19. John Loder of Southern Records who helped Crass with pressing and distributing their records soon started to provide the same services for Dischord Records which was experiencing cash-flow problems in the early 1980s. The relationship be-

tween Southern and Dischord continues into the present. Penny Rimbaud tells the story of Crass Records in *Shibboleth: My Revolting Life* (Edinburgh and San Francisco: AK Press, 1998), 104–25. On anarcho-punk in Britain see Ian Glasper, *The Day the Country Died* (London: Cherry Red, 2006).

20. Although this chapter describes fairly broad movements involving many people, collectives and organizations, it also is worth noting the influence of some fairly strong personalities on the emergence of the DIY punk scene. These include individuals such as Ian MacKaye (Dischord Records), Tim Yohannan (*Maximumrocknroll*), and Penny Rimbaud (Crass). In spite of the supposed impatience of punk for hippies, these three individuals were heavily influenced by the cultural revolutions of the 1960s: Yohannan and Rimbaud directly, and MacKaye through the indirect influence of his parents. Steve Tupper of Subterranean Records was also involved in the Diggers in San Francisco in the 1960s and attempted to continue this kind of community activism in the early punk scene.

CHAPTER TWO

Commercial and DIY Labels

Most books about punk attempt to defend what the writer considers to be its essential meaning. Even a discography is based on assumptions about what hardcore punk ought to sound like. In many cases these definitions are based on the writer's own experience of the scene. Those with a stake in an artistic or musical field define the field in terms of their own investments in it. So we read that punk in England ended in 1978, or that American hardcore existed from 1980 to 1986, or that punk "broke" in 1991. And to challenge these versions is often taken as personal affront. Well, were you there? Or dismissed as the personal opinion to which everyone is entitled in the letters pages of fanzines. All of this disagreement is not surprising because artistic and cultural fields always have a range of diversity. Most people have personal experience of only part of it. A sociology of punk must map this actual diversity. Bourdieu writing about art constructs diagrams of the field. It is possible to do the same for punk.

It is important to understand that these are not categories of punk. The diagram is a field of possibilities. A band can be placed (marked by a dot) anywhere on the diagram. Bands often move around the field as they change their strategy and usually also change their sound. Minor Threat goes somewhere in the youth anthems part of the diagram, but Fugazi belongs in the art punk sector. Bands on the right side of the diagram have broader appeal and often sell more records. Bands on the left side of the diagram usually have a more restricted audience, though the Dead Kennedys and Fugazi both have high sales. Bands on the right side of the diagram tend to be more politically

ART PUNK *Sonic Youth*	COMMERCIAL PUNK *The Ramones*
ANARCHO-PUNK *Crucifix*	YOUTH ANTHEMS *Youth of Today*

Figure 2.1.   The Field of Punk in the United States (1980s)

conservative, whereas those on the left usually have more radical political views. It is quite likely that a band that fits about the middle of the diagram of the field would appeal to many different people and therefore would accumulate higher sales. But the highest sales might be a band on the boundary of the fields of punk and heavy metal, such as Suicidal Tendencies.[1]

In his discussion of the artistic field in France about 1860, Bourdieu makes a distinction between large-scale production and small-scale production. His example of large-scale production is theater in Paris when a lot of money could be quickly made from writing a successful play. Since the main audience for theater was well-off people who could afford an expensive evening of entertainment it is unlikely that there would be many radical ideas in these plays (there was sometimes satire of bourgeois values). Bourdieu's example of small-scale production is experimental poetry that was basically just read by other poets. This is what you read today in university literature courses. When it was published there was no money to be made from writing experimental poetry. A novelist might be able to live from their work, though a private income always helps. *Sentimental Education* was not successful during Flaubert's lifetime.

The mainstream music industry in the 1960s and 1970s was all about large-scale production. The major record companies wanted immediate hits that would sell 500,000 copies or more. This is still the case today. After 1981 hardcore punk is mostly about small-scale production. Most records are then pressed in editions of one to five thousand copies. The situation has changed from the large-scale production of punk records by commercial record companies in the late 1970s. Joe Carducci at SST Records now despairs that no matter how hard everybody works it is impossible for a punk band to reach anywhere near 40,000 in sales. Bourdieu adds that small-scale production of art tends to involve younger people, or to be youth-oriented. This was certainly true for hardcore punks, who tended to be much younger than the first wave of punk bands in 1977.

In the small-scale sector of cultural fields the rewards are not immediate economic success. In fact, most people have to support their artistic activities in others ways. In France in the 1860s artists and writers who spurned the immediate cash of large-scale production either had to live on a private income from their family or live a low-cost Bohemian life. There is a sharp contrast between the respectable middle class and those living this rebellious lifestyle.

> All of this is no less true of its most destitute members who, strong in their cultural capital and the authority of being *taste-makers*, succeed in providing themselves at the least cost with audacities of dress, culinary fantasies, mercenary loves and refined leisure, for all of which the "bourgeois" pay dearly.[2]

This description of nineteenth-century Bohemia sounds surprisingly familiar. Today in the punk scene many people support their activities with day jobs (family allowances seem to have gone out of style) and by living much the same low-cost punk lifestyle. Bourdieu points out that one of the functions of a Bohemian way of life is that people tend to get social support from others who are doing the same thing. If all of your friends buy their clothes at Goodwill, drive a $500 dollar car (or live downtown and use their bikes), it is much easier to live on a tiny income. People with free time can also find or create interesting places to socialize. It might be a café in Paris, a punk house in Washington, DC, or a cheap bar on the Lower East Side. These are places to hang out, to meet people you might work with in the future, and to get support for opting out of normal middle-class life. It might sometimes be tough, but it could even be fun. This kind of social support allows people to make music that has little or no immediate commercial appeal. Most of us call this the punk scene.[3]

In the early years, big bands such as Black Flag and the Dead Kennedys operated in ways that today seem quite commercial. Ruth Schwartz wrote an article in *Maximumrocknroll* in 1982 titled "Warning! This Label May Be Hazardous To Your Health."[4] She makes the now-familiar argument that punk that is anti-authority and against big business should not be on a major label. If you press one to two thousand copies it costs only about $1.25 to make an LP. At the time, albums sold for five or six dollars. How much of this do the bands ever see? But many so-called independent labels operate no differently from the majors. In 1982 labels such as 415, Stiff and I.R.S. actually have manufacturing and distribution deals with major labels. They are acting as little more than talent scouts for them. Schwartz goes on to criticize Alternative Tentacles for not doing their own production but farming this out

Table 2.1. Punk Record Labels: Into the 1980s

Record Label	Place	Year	Founders	Related Band
UNITED STATES				
SST	Long Beach, CA	1978	Greg Ginn	Black Flag
Twin / Tone	Minneapolis	1978	Peter Jesperson, Paul Stark, Charley Hallman	none
Alternative Tentacles	San Francisco	1979	Jello Biafra	Dead Kennedys
Subterranean	San Francisco	1979	Steve Tupper	The Flying Fucks
Dischord	Washington, DC	1980	Ian MacKaye, Jeff Nelson	Teen Idles, Minor Threat
New Alliance	San Pedro, CA	1980	D. Boon, Mike Watt, Martin Tamburovich	The Minutemen
Reflex Records	Minneapolis	1981	Bob Mould, Grant Hart	Hüsker Dü
Touch & Go	Detroit, Chicago	1981	Tesco Vee, Corey Rusk	Meatmen, Necros
Taang!	Boston	1981	Curtis Casella	Legend
R Radical	San Francisco	1982	Dave Dictor	MDC
UNITED KINGDOM				
Factory Records	Manchester	1978	Tony Wilson, Alan Erasmus	none
Rough Trade	London	1978	Geoff Travis	none
Southern Records	London	1978	John Loder	Exit (1970–74)
Crass Records	London	1979	Collective	Crass
Riot City	Bristol	1981	Simon Edwards	
CANADA				
Sudden Death	Vancouver	1978	Joey Keithly	D.O.A.
Fringe Product	Toronto	1981	Ben Hoffman	none

Note: Although there is no recording available from Steve Tupper's band The Flying Fucks, it is clear from Interview no. 47 that he is a 1960s-style cultural activist turned punk. Asked about Subterranean Records he grins and says that it is not a business. It is not a business at all.

to Faulty Records, who pattern themselves after major labels.[5] Y America has a similar relationship with Important. She ends by making a case for truly alternative record labels. This includes bands that put out their own records but also labels such as Subterranean, Thermador, Touch & Go, Dischord, Rough Trade, New Alliance, SST, Modern Method and C.I.A. These are the real alternatives to capitalism in the record industry.

In Britain the field was somewhat different. Crass Records, Rough Trade, and Factory Records were explicitly "political" in how they operated. Crass insisted on low-cost records, Rough Trade operated as collective, and Factory offered bands a 50:50 split of revenue after expenses. Other labels such as Riot City behaved more like ordinary businesses.[6] Factory Records and Rough Trade released post-punk bands such as New Order and the Smiths. Southern Records was closely allied with Crass Records (and other independent labels including Dischord) and was closer to the DIY practices being developed in the US. Riot City was one of the labels releasing street punk bands such as Chaos UK and the Varukers in the early 1980s. Whereas the leading DIY punk labels in the USA in the early 1980s were sometimes associated with well-known bands, in Britain they tended to be operated by industry people. The founders of Factory records were Tony Wilson, a TV presenter, and Alan Erasmus who worked as a band manager. Simon Edwards is described as a local musician and manager. John Loder of Southern Records was a recording engineer, though he also played in an experimental band in the early 1970s. The smaller size of Great Britain and the centralization of the mass media in London are significant factors. An indication of the size of the audience for punk in the UK at this time is that the first Dead Kennedys's album on Cherry Red sold 20,000 copies in one week when it was released in 1980. The second album by Crass, *Stations of the Crass* (1979) also sold 20,000 copies within two weeks. The UK Subs at the crest of the first wave of punk in England sold about 75,000 copies.[7]

In Canada, Sudden Death on the west coast was similar to Alternative Tentacles, but on a much smaller scale. Fringe Product in Toronto was a record store and licenced albums by bands like Hüsker Dü and the Dead Kennedys for release in Canada. Fringe Product was also for a time the Canadian distributor for *Maximumrocknroll.*

Punk labels such as SST and Alternative Tentacles soon seemed quite large.[8] The wave of hardcore punk in the early 1980s gave rise to many small labels that existed for a year or two, issued eight or ten records and then disappeared. Among these are Risky Records in San Francisco, which issued two records by Toxic Reasons. Smoke Seven Records in Reseda, California issued about a dozen records from 1981 to 1983, including an album by Red

Cross and a split LP with Genocide and MIA. C.I.A. Records in Houston went for a little longer, putting out records by Really Red and other bands. Some labels such as X-Claim in Boston and Ruthless Records in Chicago were only a name used by different local bands to release their own records. SS Decontrol appeared on the X-Claim label and the Effigies and Big Black on Ruthless. There were many small hardcore labels in the early 1980s that today are known only by record collectors.

In the mid-1980s it was fairly common for a band to release their own recording, especially on cassette. About 1985 there was a noticeable increase in bands advertising their own recordings in *Maximumrocknroll*. The band Angry Red Planet from Michigan shared this attitude with many others.

> We just thought we should get a record out before we'd been together for a year, and decided that no one else was going to do it. If we had waited for someone else, we'd still be waiting. We had four songs we thought were really solid and a good introduction to the band. We didn't plan on breaking even; just wanted to make a swell first impression. We sold a thousand, and it got good reviews everywhere. . . .[9]

Following this they had a 7" record released by Touch & Go. Bands in other parts of the world such as Brazil, Italy, Holland and even Scotland, probably had little other choice but to release their cassettes and records themselves. They would sell them at shows and by mail-order and through different punk distributors.

There were small record labels all over the United States that were closely associated with a punk band. Adrenalin O.D. had Buy Our Records, which released their own material and soon became an important New Jersey hardcore label. Mail orders were not processed when Adrenalin O.D. went on tour! In 1985 the label was distributed by Important, Rough Trade, Systematic, Dutch East, and Toxic Shock. Ax/ction Records in Boston was associated with the band Psycho and released their material as well as other bands such as Cancerous Growth, mainly from about 1983 to the early 1990s.[10] Placebo Records in Phoenix, Arizona existed from about 1981 to 1988 and was associated with the band JFA. Positive Force Records was the record label of 7 Seconds and operated from about 1984 to 1987. The legendary Pusmort Records was active from about 1984 to 1988 and was run by Brian "Pushead" Schroeder, singer in the band Septic Death. He was also a writer for *Maximumrocknroll* and is a well-known artist and illustrator.[11]

Somewhat different is a fairly large label like Mystic Records, operated by Doug Moody in California. He had a background in the music industry and got interested in hardcore bands through a friend. Mystic released many punk records and is associated especially with hardcore bands in the Los Angeles area from the early 1980s. In the mid-1980s the Washington D.C. band Government Issue also had several vinyl releases on Mystic. The records were often pressed in editions of one or two thousand and bands were paid only in copies, 10 percent of the pressing. Some bands also complained that Moody put out a lot of records but did little to promote them. Maybe in response to this he started to release label samplers. The Mystic Record Group was a regular advertiser in *Maximumrocknroll*. Mixed feelings about the label are perhaps expressed by the title of a 7" record by NOFX, *So What If We're On Mystic!* (1986).[12]

While many bands continued to release their own records or were on independent punk labels, others were seeking to move up. The New York hardcore band Rest in Pieces advertised their four-song EP in *Maximumrocknroll* in November 1985. It was available by mail order and distributed by Rough Trade and Systematic. In 1987 they released an LP also on a small label. But by 1990 they graduated to Roadracer / Roadrunner Records. Members of this band later played in the well-known hardcore band Sick of it All.

The prime example of a band moving to a major label in the 1980s is Hüsker Dü. The fast but melodic punk band from Minneapolis released its first single on its own Reflex Records, with distribution by Systematic. It was then on Mike Watt's New Alliance label and soon picked up by SST. Initial pressings had gone from 2,000 to 5,000 copies that were quickly sold out. Although it had some political leanings, DIY was more of a necessity than a core belief and a few years later the band made the leap to Warner Bros. In an interview in *Maximumrocknroll* in February 1986, Bob Mould says what just about every band says in this situation. Hüsker Dü has complete artistic control: there will be no change in songs or artwork to suit Warner Bros. The band had been criticized, especially on its recent European tour, for not making political statements. But they don't feel qualified to speak on subjects about which they have little knowledge. As far as "selling out" goes, some booking companies are worse than major labels.[13] It might have been better had Mould talked more openly about some of the positive and negative aspects of working with an independent label. The band was surprisingly loyal to SST even though the label was sometimes unable to press enough records to meet demand. There were also some differences in values between band and label. What did the band want to achieve? Were there other options besides signing with a major? Ruth Schwartz wrote a letter in the next issue of *Maximumrocknroll* in which she points out that punk labels and distributors will always be weakened if well-known bands such as Hüsker Dü, Dead Kennedys, Black Flag, and D.O.A. sign with major labels. The success of these bands and their relatively high sales are crucial to the future of the underground labels and independent distributors. Tim Yohannan added a note saying that he agreed.[14]

The late 1980s then saw the emergence of a new generation of grassroots punk entrepreneurs.[15] Although many of these labels are associated with famous bands it sometimes turns out that the musician soon drops out of the picture. The charismatic Ray Cappo founded two records labels and quickly left them for others to continue operating. Larry Livermore and Dirk Hemsath were both in bands, but this is completely overshadowed by their subsequent careers as businessmen (and in Livermore's case as a writer). Vinnie Fiorello of Less Than Jake is no longer involved in the operation of Fueled By Ramen. It should also be noted that many of these commercial record labels predate the major-label punk explosion of the early 1990s. Nirvana's album *Nevermind* was released in 1991 on Geffen / DGC (owned by major label MCA, later renamed Universal Music Group). Within six months it sold 3 million copies. This provoked a wave of interest in punk and bands inspired by punk sounds. Three soon had huge sales: The Offspring with *Smash*, Green Day with *Dookie*, and NOFX with *Punk in Drublic*.[16]

These commercial punk labels are not all the same but they do have some characteristics in common.[17] They are not operated by music industry professionals, sometimes carelessly defined as guys with good haircuts. These people are generally in their thirties (Livermore is somewhat older) and grew up on punk rock. They were part of the scene and friends with bands. Some were in punk bands themselves and others went on tour with bands as roadies. Almost none of these people have any formal business training. The exception to this (John Janick) was operating the label for years before he got his MBA degree. All of these people learned how to run a record label by doing it themselves. Although they may be small by the standards of the music industry, these are at times highly successful record labels. Although punk rock is mainly a niche market, some of these labels have released records that have gone gold (500,000 sales of an album in the United States).

The debate about punk bands moving from the underground to major labels gained steam in the early 1990s. There were basically two arguments. The first is that the vast majority of bands do poorly on major labels. In a famous article reprinted in the *Maximumrocknroll* special issue on Major Labels in June 1994, Steve Albini gave figures for a band that sells 250,000 copies of an album. Because of the high costs of working within the industry, Albini's figures show that the band would make about $16,000 in profit, about $4,000 per band member. A tiny number of bands like Green Day make much more than this. But most of the bands such as Jawbox, which left

Table 2.2. Commercial Punk labels (late 1980s–1990s)

Record Label	Place	Year	Founders	Related Band
Epitaph	Hollywood, CA	1987	Brett Gurewitz	Bad Religion
Lookout!	Berkeley, CA	1987	Larry Livermore, David Hayes	The Lookouts
New Red Archives	New York, San Francisco	1987	Nicky Garrett	UK Subs
Revelation	New Haven, CN	1987	Ray Cappo, Jordan Cooper	Youth of Today
Doghouse	Toledo, OH	1988	Dirk Hemsath	Majority of One
Victory	Chicago	1989	Tony Brummel	
Fat Wreck Chords	San Francisco	1990	Fat Mike, Erin Burkett	NOFX
Equal Vision	Albany, NY	1992	Ray Cappo, Steve Reddy	Shelter
Hopeless	Van Nuys, CA	1993	Louis Posen	none
Nitro Records	Huntington Beach, CA	1995	Dexter Holland	The Offspring
Fueled by Ramen	Gainesville, FL	1996	Vinnie Fiorello, John Janick	Less Than Jake

Note: Epitaph Records had its first release in 1980 but did not really operate as a record label until 1987.

Dischord Records to sign with Atlantic, came to regret their decision to sign with a major label. The second argument made by commentators in *Maximumrocknroll* has to do with the autonomy of the scene. Successful bands have been made possible in part by a nonprofit infrastructure such as *Maximumrocknroll*, community spaces such as Gilman Street, and the unpaid work of show promoters, zine publishers, people who host punk shows on community radio, DIY record labels and distributors. Not to mention the enthusiastic support of idealistic kids who come to shows. If successful bands simply leave this underground for the major labels the autonomy of the entire field is weakened. Imagine if these bands instead used their popularity to strengthen independent labels and their distributors, independent promoters and community spaces, zines and the whole punk underground.[18]

The 1990s equivalent of Hüsker Dü was Green Day. Except there was even less excuse for Green Day because the band grew up and was nurtured within the non-profit and politically-conscious punk scene based in the San Francisco area. The band members were exposed to the music scene and its ethics at the Gilman Street community center. This is also where the band played its first shows. The thank-you list for *Kerplunk!* reads like a who's who of the East Bay punk community in 1991, including Gilman Street and Tim Yohannan. The band was friends with Aaron Cometbus whose zine is testimony for a low-budget lifestyle, the values of friendship and punk community. Green Day released *39/Smooth* and *Kerplunk!* on Lookout! Records, part-owned by MRR columnist Larry Livermore who had also encouraged the band from the beginning. But with the music industry in overdrive following the commercial success of Nirvana, there were now other possibilities. The band members hired Cahnman Management in 1992 to commercialize their career. Band manager and lawyer Jeff Saltzman and Elliott Cahn were soon marketing Green Day to major labels on the basis of 30,000 sales for both albums released in the underground punk scene.[19]

The field of punk labels in the 1990s has a dual structure. The other side to the commercial punk labels is a quite extraordinary wave of DIY punk labels that are each associated with a popular underground band. Unlike punk bands in the 1980s, these bands were part of a more hospitable underground for touring bands. There were fewer concerts in clubs and more all-ages shows organized by local punk kids. There were fewer meals at Burger King and more homemade meals of pasta and tomato sauce. Bands still slept on the floor but were more likely to stay up for hours talking with their punk hosts.[20] If it was not possible to make a living from being in a hardcore band, sometimes the additional income from running a record label meant that the person doing it did not have to work a day job. Other times the label lost money and had to be supported by working two day jobs.

Whereas one looks in vain for any serious political involvement in the commercial punk labels of the late 1980s and early 1990s (there is occasional community service or an effort to get punks to register to vote), many of the new DIY punk labels have well-defined political profiles. And although there are still few women running punk record labels, we begin to see more substantial involvement of women in labels like Simple Machines, Six Weeks and Three One G.[21]

These record labels were made possible in part because of the expansion of the punk scene in the 1990s. There were actually so many new punk labels that *Maximumrocknroll* had trouble fitting in all the advertisements, even though by 1995 the largest ad size permitted was one-third of a page. Many of the new record labels disappeared by the late 1990s. Tim Yohannan complained that half of them were operating like commercial record labels. But that also means that half of them were not. Simple Machines was started in 1990 and wound up in 1998 when the decline in interest made it more difficult to run a punk label. Six Weeks, which is associated with fast and loud hardcore, started in 1992. Gold Standard Laboratories which is located more in the art punk scene began the following year. Some labels are distributed through Mordam (Asian Man, Broken Records, Six Weeks, Sound Pollution, Vermiform) or through the Dischord Records and Southern distribution arrangement (Simple Machines, Slowdime Records). For many labels even this was too commercial. They preferred to use a number of smaller punk distributors and to trade records with other DIY labels around the world. For some, this autonomous network was regarded as central to the activity of doing the label. (Mordam would sometimes allow these relationships to continue. Ken Pollution was allowed to keep his international trading partners.)

The two sectors of the field operate in distinct ways. The line between them is not as simple as low prices for records or refusing to print bar codes on releases. It is not simply a matter of a preference for vinyl over CDs. The whole set of practices taken together are distinct. Commercial punk labels usually have a small warehouse with office space. They have anywhere from six to twenty employees (or more). With this kind of responsibility, they explain, it is necessary to have signed legal contracts with the bands. These contracts are usually based on a points system the same as major label contracts, though the terms of the contracts are often more reasonable. Bands sometimes receive advances of amounts from $5,000 to $50,000. Records and CDs are pressed in batches of 5,000 copies and the label expects regular sales

Table 2.3. The Decade of DIY: Bands and Associated Labels (1990s)

Record label	Place	Founders	Band
625 Thrash	San Francisco	Max Ward	Spazz
Asian Man	Monte Serano, CA	Mike Park	Skankin' Pickle
Broken Rekids / Records	San Francisco	Mike Millett	A.P.P.L.E.
Council Records	Dearborn, MI; Phoenix, AZ	Matt Weeks	Current
Crimethinc	Atlanta, GA; Olympia, WA	Brian / collective	Catharsis
Deep Six	Burbank, CA	Bob Deep Six	Lack of Interest
Donut Friends	Kent, OH	Jamie Stillman	Harriet The Spy
G-7 Welcoming Committee	Winnipeg	collective	Propagandhi
Gloom Records	Albany, NY	Nate Wilson	Devoid of Faith
Gold Standard Laboratories	Boulder, CO; San Diego, CA	Sonny Kay	Angel Hair
Gravity	San Diego	Matt Anderson	Heroin
Great American Steak Religion	St-Romuald, PQ; Ottawa, ON	Yannick	Union of Uranus
Havoc	Minneapolis	Felix Havoc	Destroy, Code-13
Lengua Armada	Chicago, San Francisco	Martín Sorrondeguy	Los Crudos
Mountain	Huntington, NY	Chris Jensen	Halfman
No Idea	Gainesville, FL	Var Thelin	Bombshell
Old Glory Records	Brattleboro, VT	Kevin Cebrese	Iconoclast
Recess Records	Torrance, CA	Todd Congelliere	F.Y.P., Toys That Kill
Simple Machines	Arlington, VA	Jenny Toomey, Kristin Thompson	Tsunami
Six Weeks Records	Cotati, CA	Athena Krautsch, Jeff Robinson	The Dread, Capitalist Casualties
Slap A Ham	San Francisco	Chris Dodge	Spazz
Slowdime Records	Washington DC	Juan Luis Carrera, John Wall	Warmers, Kerosene 454
Burrito / Sound Idea	Brandon, FL	Bob Suren	Flaming Midget, Failure Face
Sound Pollution	Covington, KY	Ken Pollution	Hellnation
Three One G	San Diego	Justin Pearson, Allysia Edwards	The Locust
Tribal War Records	New York; Portland, OR	Neil	Nausea
Verniform	Richmond, VA	Sam McPheeters	Born Against

of 20,000 to 100,000 copies. This requires an investment in promotion, often employing small outside companies that specialize in this. Some of these labels pay to have their bands participate in the Warped Tour or Ozzfest, and then pay for the tour bus. The sales necessary to sustain all this usually require distribution through one of the major-label subsidiaries (Fontana, ADA, RED or Caroline). Once this relationship with the major corporation is in place there is occasionally an agreement that the most successful bands will be upstreamed to an imprint owned by the major label itself. Every record label owner says that the reason they do it is that they love the music. There is no reason to doubt this, but these commercial punk labels are also businesses.

If the record label has an office / warehouse it is in a light industrial park or commercial area along with car body shops, glass repair, lawnmower shops, air conditioning services and some light industry. Perhaps there is a nearby seedy bar ("Girls") or in California there is a Mexican restaurant where not much English is spoken. Record labels never have a prominent sign, or even any sign at all on the building. Musicians used to the back entrances of clubs may feel at home but it is far from the glamorous image of the recording industry.[22]

The DIY sector is quite different. It is often operated from a musician's house (the basement, a spare room, even a closet) and often shares the same phone line. The label is usually done by one or two people. The bands are friends and there is no question of legal contracts. Most of these labels only release bands that they personally know. Records and CDs are pressed in batches of 1,000 or 2,000. Bands are paid with copies of records (15 percent to 20 percent), and sometimes there is a 50:50 split of profits after all expenses have been paid. Done in this way albums can break even after 2,000 copies (less for CDs because they are cheaper to produce). The number of review copies sent to zines, websites and college radio stations varies between zero and 500 copies. DIY punk labels occasionally hire freelance promotion companies. Everyone who runs a DIY punk label also says they love the music. Some also mention the importance of a social network, friends they have made, just being part of the scene.

It is possible for a record label to cross over between the two sectors of the field. This can go both ways. An interesting example is Asian Man. It has always been a small label but in the beginning it was run in a professional way with good distribution through Mordam and a lot of emphasis on promotion until Mike Park decided that he actually preferred to do things on a small scale. (His website explains that the label runs out of his parents' garage. It is actually a *double* garage.) Jade Tree in Wilmington, Delaware, occupies a

Table 2.4.   Highest Sales and Review Copies for Commercial and DIY Labels

Commercial Label	Highest Sales	Review Copies	DIY Label	Highest Sales	Review Copies
BYO	225,000	1000	A Wrench in the Gears	1,200	10
Doghouse	150,000	500	Ebullition	13,000	0
Equal Vision	500,000	2000	Gloom	7,500	5
Fueled By Ramen	500,000	500	Havoc	25,000	100
Hopeless	340,000	1500	Lengua Armada	17,000	10
Jade Tree	100,000	400	Punks Before Profits	1,500	8
New Red Archives	100,000	750	Sound Pollution	16,000	50
Revelation	100,000	150	Schitzophrenic	2,000	5

Source: Interviews with record labels. The sales figure for Doghouse is low because successful bands on this label are upstreamed to imprints of major labels. All American Rejects sold a million and a half copies of their first album on Dreamworks (Universal Music Group). BYO sends out between 500 and 2000 promotion copies. Ebullition sends out none at all.

fairly unique position between commercial and DIY labels. However, with the sale of Mordam the record label switched to distribution with an older but compatible label. Touch & Go is distributed by ADA (Warner Music Group) and Jade Tree now occupies a position closer to a commercial punk label like Equal Vision.[23]

It is not easy to make a record label work. In both the commercial and the DIY punk sectors labels look to other activities to help pay the bills. Matt Anderson at Gravity Records operated a recording studio for a number of years. Equal Vision has a substantial silk-screen operation that supplies bands with t-shirts and it also markets them through its Merch Now website. Hopeless Records in California operates downloadpunk.com, specializing in electronic sales of punk music. Dirtnap Records survives in part as a retail store in Portland, Oregon. Discourage Records is also a mail order for rare punk vinyl. Burrito Records is part of Sound Idea distribution and record store in Brandon, Florida. Some record labels also operate as distributors.

Notes

1. Correspondence analysis is a statistical method for showing relations in a set of complex data. It does not show that A was caused by B but that there is a relation between them. Correspondence analysis is done with a computer program that is somewhat like a spread sheet. It produces diagrams of the field that place similar cases close and dissimilar ones far away. The diagrams resemble music-maps that are available online except that in this case they are based on statistical variables chosen by the researcher and not individual preferences for music as at http://www .music-map.com (29 June 2007). Bourdieu occasionally does an informal diagram of

correspondences based on his knowledge of the field rather than a set of statistics. (He does this for the literary field in nineteenth-century France.) To construct an informal diagram of the field of punk based on your record collection you would not sort the records into crates based on categories (city, label, thrash, pop punk) but instead place them one by one on the floor like pieces on a giant chessboard. As you place each record down you must determine its position in relation to every one of the records already spread out on the floor. Each time you add a record you alter the whole field.

2. Pierre Bourdieu, *The Rules of Art: Genesis and Structure of the Literary Field*, trans. Susan Emanuel (Stanford: Stanford University Press, 1996), 57.

3. One sign of a bohemian lifestyle is that a relatively small number of people interviewed for this book have children. Iñaki says: "Of course, of course. I don't have any children. I'm twenty-eight [. . .] I don't plan to have children. I have to become clearer about my life in many aspects. To have a child, to have that responsibility, because I think that's the biggest responsibility you can have." (Interview no. 1, with La Idea)

4. Ruth Schwartz, "Warning! This Label May Be Hazardous To Your Health," *Maximumrocknroll* no. 2, September–October 1982, 2 pages. See also East Bay Ray, "Vinyl Economics," *Maximumrocknroll* no. 6, May–June 1983, 1 page. He argues that middleman labels like Faulty Products can get a band better distribution and what matters is not the type of deal offered but the people at the label. Available online at www.operationphoenix.com (24 April 2007).

5. For example, D.O.A. *War on 45* (Virus 24) on Alternative Tentacles was manufactured by Faulty Products in 1982. Other labels such as Cabbage Records, which issued three recordings by Kraut in 1981–1982, were also manufactured and distributed by Faulty.

6. Simon Edwards was friends with the band Vice Squad. Boffo from Chumbawamba complains in a letter to *Maximumrocknroll* that Riot City is just a tiny branch of EMI. *Maximumrocknroll* no. 9, October–November 1983. Available online at www.operationphoenix.com (24 April 2007).

7. Penny Rimbaud, "Crass Records," online at www.southern.com (17 February 2007). Sales figure for UK Subs are from interview no. 43, with New Red Archives.

8. By the mid-1980s it was quite common to make a distinction between commercial punk record labels and those that operated in a more underground way. The distinction was often based on price. But an article in *Maximumrocknroll* in 1986 on college radio stations also reported that independent labels like Enigma and SST were pushing their product using the same strategies as Warner and RCA. David Ciaffardina, "U.S.: College Radio Crumbling?" *Maximumrocknroll* no. 34, March 1986, 3 pages. Available online at www.operationphoenixrecords.com (27 April 2007). In July 1986, MRR changed its layout to separate ads from editorial content. The blocks of half-page ads from record labels, each with significant numbers of releases, now became visible as an independent or underground economy that had grown substantially over the past five years.

9. David Viecelli, interview with Angry Red Planet, *Maximumrocknroll* no. 28, September 1985, 1 page. Available online at www.operationphoenixrecords.com (26 April 2007).

10. See interview with Ax/ction Records, *Maximumrocknroll* no. 46, March 1987, 1 page. Although they took regular half-page ads in MRR this was actually a small DIY label based in the Boston area that liked to deal directly with stores and trade with distributors in Europe. The label was active from 1983 to 1991, releasing cassettes and about 15 records.

11. Pushead did the front cover for one of the best issues of *Maximumrocknroll*, no. 8, September 1983. Among his other contributions to the magazine is an article "How To Make A Record," *Maximumrocknroll* no. 21, January 1985, 3 pages. Available online www.operationphoenixrecords.com (26 April 2007).

12. There were also labels associated with indie music distributors. Enigma Records was started by Greenworld Distribution (it was distributed by Capital EMI from 1986 and a few years later bought by the major label). Dutch East India Distribution owned Braineater Records.

Maximumrocknroll sometimes reviewed records released by Homestead, a record label associated with the distribution company Dutch East India Trading. The label tended to advertise in *Flipside*, which had a broader scope than MRR. For an overview of Homestead Records see Matthew Fritch, "Frontier Days," *Magnet* no. 72, July–August 2006, 76–83. For Big Black's problems with Homestead and Dutch East India see Michael Azerrad, *Our Band Could Be Your Life: Scenes from the American Indie Underground 1981–1991* (Boston: Little Brown and Company, 2001), 335. In the late 1980s, Dutch East was doing press and distribution deals with labels including Giant, Positive Force and Flipside Records. See editorial response to a letter in *Maximumrocknroll* no. 57, January 1988, 1 page. Available online at www.operation phoenixrecords.com (30 April 2007).

13. "What th' Fuck!" interview with Bob Mould, *Maximumrocknroll* no. 33, February 1986, 2 pages. Available online www.operationphoenixrecords.com (accessed 27 April 2007). According to Michael Azerrad, from its beginning in 1979, the band had ambitions to be on Sire Records like the Ramones. *Our Band Could Be Your Life*, 161. The debut album on Warner Bros. got a lukewarm review by Tim Yohannan in *Maximumrocknroll* no. 36, May 1986. The label was listed as "some multinational corporation."

14. Much of the discussion about bands "selling out" in the 1980s was not about record labels but about bands playing over-priced shows and demanding large guarantees. For critical commentary on this see "What the Fuck," interview with MDC in *Maximumrocknroll* no. 42, November 1986, 4 pages. And interview with BGK, *Maximumrocknroll* no. 43, December 1986, 2 pages. Available online at www .operationphoenixrecords.com (29 April 2007). It was alleged that big bands such as Dead Kennedys, Black Flag, Circle Jerks and Bad Brains were asking for as much as $3,000 to $6,000 per show. Presumably this is for bigger concerts. In 1987 bands like

Circle Jerks or DRI attracted 200–300 people in a city like Buffalo. (The 924 Gilman Street community space in Berkeley opened as an alternative to commercial venues at this time.) The issue of record labels gradually emerged in print in MRR in the late 1980s. See the discussion with Chris Bald and Thomasso which includes some unusually blunt opinions about Dischord, SST, Enigma, Dutch East and Alchemy, in *Maximumrocknroll* no. 66, November 1988, 4 pages. Even the January 1992 special issue on Punk Business was mainly about bands and concert prices. See Ben Weasel, "The Business of Punk Rock," 8 pages, and Tim Yohannan, interview with Fugazi, 6 pages, in *Maximumrocknroll* no. 104, January 1992.

15. Kent McClard comments on the difference between DIY punk in the 1980s and the 1990s: "The one thing I didn't like about the eighties straightedge scene is that it didn't have a DIY ethic. It was more of a DIY because we have to, and not because that's fundamentally important." (Interview no. 43, with Kent McClard)

16. For commercial "neo-punk" associated with the Warped Tour and Epitaph Records see Matt Diehl, *My So-Called Punk* (New York: St. Martin's, 2007).

17. En Guard Records in Montreal was run by Paul Gott from the Ripcordz. In three years the label put out 35 records and tapes, usually in editions of 1,000 copies. But it was apparently more difficult to operate a small punk business from Canada. "We had found 2 distributors in the U.S., they said that the records were selling very well but we never see the money." Interview with En Guard Records, *Maximumrocknroll* no. 140, January 1995, 1 page.

18. These arguments about the autonomy of the field of hardcore punk were made by Samuel Nathan Schiffman, "Nirvanification: The Death of the Rock Underground," *Maximumrocknroll* no. 110, July 1992, 4 pages, and by many of the contributors to the Major Labels special issue of *Maximumrocknroll* no. 133, June 1994. *Flipside* zine shared many of the same values as MRR but its writers did not challenge bands to the same extent. See Gary Indiana, "At last! The secrets of Bad Religion revealed!," *Flipside* no. 88, February–March 1994, 2 pages. The interviewer asks about the band signing to Atlantic but does not really challenge Brett Gurewitz's cynicism that the band deserves criticism for selling out and that he is only doing it for the money. It is interesting to imagine the kind of questions that Tim Yohannan would have asked the band which in 1991 released a 7" record on the Maximumrocknroll record label, with spoken work by Noam Chomsky, to protest the Gulf War. See Tim's "Yo Mama" column and the "Far Enough" column by Adrienne Droogas in *Maximumrocknroll* no. 141, February 1995, both 2 pages. Adrienne's band Spitboy turned down an invitation to play with the Offspring.

19. Marc Spitz, *Nobody Likes You: Inside the Turbulent Life, Times, and Music of Green Day* (New York: Hyperion, 2006) gives sales figures of 30,000 copies of each album on Lookout! Records when they signed with Reprise/Warner in 1993 (p. 81). He bases this on a story in the *San Francisco Chronicle*, 24 August 1993. Ben Myers, *Green Day: American Idiots & the New Punk Explosion* (New York: Disinformation, 2006, 91) also reports that by Spring 1993 the band had sold a total of 60,000 copies. By the end

of 1995 the two albums on Lookout! had sold more than 500,000 each in the United States. Part of the Green Day story is the way in which this commercialization of the underground punk scene affected Larry Livermore, whose business behavior was soon being publicly criticized by bands as well as by Tim Yohannan. For George Tabb's experience with Lookout! see his column in *Maximumrocknroll* no. 165, February 1997, 5 pages and for Tim Yohannan's bitter criticism of Livermore, his column in the same issue, 1 page. For Ben Weasel's expose of Lookout! see *Maximumrocknroll* no. 168, May 1997, 5 pages. Livermore sold his share in the record label in 1997 and retired a wealthy man. Many of the bands, including Green Day later sued the new owners to regain their recordings, because the company is unable to pay royalties. The label no longer has major-label distribution. It is a sad trail of broken friendships, aggressive business tactics and abandoned ideals.

20. The classic document of a 1980s touring band is the video *Another State of Mind*, Peter Stuart and Adam Small, New York, Time Bomb Films, 1983. The highlights of the film are the arrival of the bands at punk houses in the United States and Canada but in between were long stretches of playing at clubs and sleeping in the bus. The harsh conditions for a touring band in the 1980s are described in Joe Cole, *Planet Joe* (Los Angeles: 2.13.61., 1992) and in Henry Rollins, *Get in the Van: On the Road with Black Flag* (Los Angeles: 2.13.61, 1994). See also Mike Watt, *Spiels of a Minuteman* (Montreal: L'Oie de Sravan, 2003). More of a grassroots infrastructure emerged in the following decade. See Jon Resh, *Amped: Notes From a Go-Nowhere Punk Band* (Chicago: Viper Press, 2001).

21. The label manager at Chunksaah Records is the very wonderful Kate Hiltz. But even she ruefully explains that she is often known in the punk scene as Jon Hiltz's sister. Jon Hiltz is a musician and played drums in Born Against. He is also known for doing sound at concerts in Philadelphia and before that for having punk shows at his house in New Jersey. The head of Southern Records in the United States is also a woman, Allison Schnackenberg.

22. The social geography of punk labels may be observed by a comparison of two states such as California and Ohio. California has about three times the population but more than five times the number of punk bands and seven times the number of record labels.

Table 2.5.   Punk Scenes in Ohio and California (1995)

	Ohio	California
Bands	36	204
Promoters and venues	6	39
Record labels	10	70
Population (in millions)	10.8	29.7

Source: *Book Your Own Fucking Life*, no. 4 (1995). Population figures for 1990 are from *The New York Times Almanac*, 2005.

23. One of the difficulties of the sale of Mordam to Lumberjack is Dirk Hemsath's contractual relationship with WEA (Warner Music Group). The amalgamation immediately put DIY labels such as Asian Man, Six Weeks and Sound Pollution in an awkward position. If *Maximumrocknroll* strictly enforced its no major-label affiliation policy after 2005 it would not be able to accept ads from these labels. MRR has been quietly accepting some ads that previously might have been rejected.

CHAPTER THREE

The Problem of Distribution

In the 1980s punk record labels were usually distributed in the United States by several independent distributors such as Dutch East India Trading, Faulty, Greenworld, Important, Jem, Rough Trade, Systematic and Twin Cities. These businesses provided an infrastructure, even if at times they caused huge problems. Distributors went bankrupt or created difficulties by not paying on time or with questionable accounting practices. Punk record labels had little choice if they wanted to get their records into stores. They had to use these companies because they did not have direct access to major-label distributors. Bands like Black Flag, the Dead Kennedys, and MDC struggled to keep their independence but also get access to good distribution. It mostly worked out quite badly. Record labels including SST, Alternative Tentacles and Subterranean were distributed by Faulty Products, an independent company owned by Miles Axe Copeland, who also owned I.R.S. Records (which was in turn distributed by a major label after February 1979). When I.R.S. pulled the plug in 1983 and Faulty Products declared bankruptcy, the small labels it distributed were badly burned.[1] The same year saw the crash of Bonaparte, Disc Trading, Sky Disc Distributors and the much larger Pickwick. The failures of these distributors caused financial problems for labels that typically had products with them on 60-day consignment. The labels' problems in turn affected payments to bands.[2]

The commercial punk labels that emerged in the 1980s and 1990s are attempting to regularly achieve sales of 20,000 to 100,000 copies. In order to

Table 3.1.   Major Label Indie Distribution (2006)

Major Label	Indie Distribution Company	Punk Labels Distributed
Universal Music Group	Fontana	BYO Records, Nitro, Punk Core, Southern Records, Taang!, Vagrant
Warner Music Group	ADA	Epitaph, Fueled By Ramen, Hopeless, Polyvinyl, Matador, Secretly Canadian (includes K Records), Side One Dummy, Sub Pop, Touch & Go
Sony BMG	RED	Equal Vision, Fat Wreck, Trustkill, Victory
EMI	Caroline	Bridge Nine, Mute

Source: This table is based on the labels listed by each distributor in July 2006. Record labels frequently change distributors. Lookout! was distributed by RED until December 2005. Revolver was listed with Caroline in 2006 but no longer sells to them. Trustkill has since moved to Fontana.

do this they try to break out of the indie record-store market and get distribution into the chain record stores. Today they will attempt to get selected releases into big-box stores like Wal-Mart. To do this it is necessary to have distribution by a major record distributor because the big retailers are not willing to deal with small independent distributors.

Record stores and distribution have seen important changes. Retail is now dominated by chains of record stores and by stores like Wal-Mart that sell CDs. Indie record stores have always been important for punk. They are not only places to buy records but also sources of information and sometimes social centers. For the twenty years after 1977 the number of Mom-and-Pop record stores increased in the United States. But because many more chain stores and big-box stores selling CDs were opened in the same period, the single-unit stores declined as a percentage of the total. According to a recent report 900 independent record stores have closed since 2003, leaving 2,700 in the United States.[3] Some of these are general record stores that cannot compete with the large chains, but there is no doubt that specialized stores that sold punk and hardcore have also been hit. As the retail industry changed it became more important for the commercial punk labels to get their records into the big stores. In the 1980s and 1990s there were different possible strategies but today you pretty much have to go through the "indie" distribution company of one of the four major labels.[4]

Following the collapse of Faulty Products in 1983, Ruth Schwartz had the idea to start an independent distributor. She had previously worked at Rough Trade. Mordam distribution was actually started with Alternative Tentacles records that were rescued from Faulty's old pressing plant. With Alternative Tentacles on board, Ruth's friend from *Maximumrocknroll* zine and radio

Table 3.2.   Independent and Chain Record Stores (USA)

Year	Mom-and-Pop	Percentage	Total Record Stores
1977	2,026	55.4	3,655
1987	2,635	42	6,272
1997	3,189	39	8,158

Source: Hull, The Recording Industry, 210–11. The figure for total record stores does not include big-box stores like Wal-Mart that sell CDs.

show, Tim Yohannan, soon decided to bring MRR over from Rough Trade as well.[5] The record labels lucky enough to be accepted by Mordam, soon had an alternative distribution network. Over time this included labels from all parts of the USA.

Mordam developed a unique model of doing business.[6] It operated like a co-operative of its record labels and a few magazines. Unlike corporate distributors, it didn't try to interfere with what the labels did. In return for exclusive distribution rights, Mordam would receive all the label's records at its warehouse on Folsom Street in San Francisco. It would take care of getting the records to other distributors, to record stores and to punk mail-order operations worldwide. The beauty of this was that Mordam could use its collective clout to actually get paid. Ruth Schwartz ran a well-organized business and the record labels got paid every month. Employees were also well-paid, received health benefits and end-of-year bonuses when Mordam did well (these could be quite substantial). Working at Mordam was soon one of the most desirable punk jobs and for many people it would be the best they ever had. There was job-sharing in that people worked both in sales and in the warehouse. There was an experiment in allowing people to work from home or even from another city, by computer, phone and fax machine. There

Table 3.3.   Mordam Distribution (1995)

Allied Recordings	Kill Rock Stars
Alternative Tentacles	Kirbdog Records
Amphetamine Reptile Records	Lookout Records
Bacchus Archives	Maximumrocknroll
Broken Records	Mordam Records
Dionysus Records	Seeland Records
Dr. Strange Records	Shredder Records
Empty Records	Sympathy for the Record Industry
Estrus Records	Verniform Records
Flipside Records	Vinyl Communications
Hell Yeah	World War 3 Illustrated Magazine
Jade Tree	Wrong Records

Source: Mordam Records, Spring 1995 Catalog

were monthly staff meetings where every employee got a vote, including on what new labels to accept into the Mordam family. There was also an annual meeting of all the record labels, often at the Mordam warehouse, to discuss issues of general concern. Naturally, it was also a social event and there was always a party with a keg of beer.[7]

As the years passed, some fundamental contradictions started to emerge. Mordam required exclusive distribution. With minor exceptions, all records had to go through the organization. If other record distributors wanted to sell Alternative Tentacles or Lookout! Records they had to buy them from Mordam. In the American economy, wholesalers sell about one-third to retailers, but two-third of their sales go to other wholesalers or manufacturers.[8] Mordam would sell records to anyone who wanted them. Tim Yohannan had brought *Maximumrocknroll* into the organization from the start. This was important because it encouraged record stores to make at least a monthly order from Mordam, to arrive along with the new issue of the magazine. Yohannan was made uncomfortable by any connection between punk rock and major record labels. This became a topic at the Mordam annual meeting in 1991 and the discussion was continued the following year. The main issue was Mordam selling through Caroline (EMI). Starting in January 1993 MRR instructed Mordam to no longer distribute the zine through Important and Caroline "since both of these entities are now owned by major labels."[9] Yohannan also blocked Mordam from distributing a zine that accepted major label advertising. Jeff Bale of *Hit List* magazine apparently wanted to accept advertising dollars from Rhino for Ramones reissues, and to accept ads for a label like Sub Pop.[10] Darren Walters remembers some of the controversies.

> There were some meetings where Tim Yohannan and Jello Biafra and Larry Livermore would argue with each other. That's the problem when you get a bunch of old punks in a room who have very significant political beliefs. They can argue about the same thing for hours on end. I remember one meeting where a decision was made, it was a pretty infamous decision at the time [about Mordam distribution with Caroline]. The big thing at the time is that Caroline was owned by Thorn-EMI and *Maximumrocknroll* said they make nukes, no way in hell, we're pulling out. That argument went on forever. For and against. (Interview no. 19, with Jade Tree)

Columnist and writer George Matiasz worked at Mordam doing invoices, reports and computers. He explains the debate at the 1992 general meeting.

> No one ever argued that Caroline should be the exclusive distributor for Mordam. That said, Caroline accounted for 60 percent to 70 percent of distribu-

tion for any given sales period. Given that reality, the divisions came down to Tim Yo pushing for a drastic cutoff of Caroline, Larry and Jello arguing for continuing things just as they were, and Ruth happy to play both sides against each other. The final compromise was to hire more sales staff and try to promote direct sales to stores, to try and whittle down Caroline's overwhelming dominance. Tim went so far, on his own, to refuse to distribute MRR, first to Dutch East, then to Caroline after that contentious meeting.[11]

At the same time, Mordam represented a certain professionalization of punk record labels. To be accepted you had to have issued a minimum number of albums and be running a fairly stable operation. The Mordam model was seen to work well and for a time it was difficult for new labels to get accepted for distribution. (In the beginning only West Coast labels were accepted but this was soon waived.) The Mordam annual meeting did not just discuss general issues. There were also rotating workshops by the Mordam staff on aspects of running a record label. They were encouraged to do one-sheets that Mordam could use to promote the record, though any kind of one-page promotion was acceptable. Labels were asked to think about foreign distribution opportunities. By the late 1990s they were even being encouraged to sign formal contracts with their bands.[12] Labels were also learning from everyday conversations with the Mordam staff. Ruth Schwartz was older than many of the new people doing labels and they looked to her as a mentor. And Ruth was a very organized and capable person.

The signing of Green Day to Warner Bros./Reprise gave a boost to the band's earlier releases. By 1994 Mordam distribution was dealing with pallets and not boxes of the Green Day records on Lookout! Records. By the end of 1995 the total sales were one million copies.[13] That and the general expansion of interest in punk music found Mordam in a much bigger warehouse space on Caeser Chavez Street, a little further out in San Francisco. Staff went from nine people in the early 1990s to twenty or twenty-five at the height of the punk explosion. The warehouse operation was streamlined by bar codes on CDs and computerized inventory. (At the same time *Heartattack* zine was refusing to review records and CDs that had bar codes printed on them.) The old DIY punk attitudes started to slip. "UPS will be here in 15 minutes, drop everything and make it happen!" There was less of that spirit as the business became more complex and also more routine. Ruth Schwartz was now working a lot from home.

The final crisis came from an unexpected direction. San Francisco was experiencing the dot-com explosion of the 1990s. People moved to San Francisco to take jobs in the "new economy" and housing soon became very difficult to

find. If rented living space was difficult, commercial property with no rent con-
trols soon became impossible.[14] The lease on the Mordam warehouse was about
to expire. At the same time, Mordam lost Lookout! Records in 2000 to RED
(Warner) soon after Larry Livermore and Patrick Hynes sold the label to employee Chris Applegren and other partners. The lawsuit brought by members
of the Dead Kennedys against Jello Biafra was decided against Alternative Tentacles. The other band members gained control of the Dead Kennedys's back
catalog and signed a deal with Manifesto Records in Los Angeles. Mordam was
faced with the loss of some of its biggest sellers. The landlord wanted to triple
the rent or take back the warehouse and break it into units for dot-com offices.
After looking around the Bay Area, Schwartz decided to move the whole operation to a smaller warehouse in Sacramento at half the rent. Many of the staff
did not make the move because they were unwilling or unable to leave San
Francisco. Mordam hired eight new employees in Sacramento. There was a
temporary drop in sales until the well-oiled organization was again running
smoothly.[15]

Meanwhile Ruth Schwartz started to take meetings with big computer
companies about paid downloads of music on the Internet. Her first response
was disbelief but she soon began to see that it was a potential challenge to
the future of record distribution. Exhausted from almost two decades of running Mordam Records, from difficult arguments with Yohannan and others,
and wanting to spend more time with her daughter, Schwartz was quietly
looking for a way out. Although it had some features of a progressive worker
co-operative, everyone there knew it was owned by Ruth Schwartz. The ob-
vious solution was to sell the business to the employees. But it was apparently
not possible for them to find the amount of money needed and this idea was
abandoned by the late 1990s. Ruth talked with Kate Hiltz (who runs
Chunksaah Records) and with Mike Park (Asian Man Records) but neither
was interested in taking on Mordam. There was apparently an inquiry to
Very Distribution in Pittsburgh, but the gossip is that those guys like to party
too much! Word began to leak out that Ruth was looking to get out of the
business. One or two labels that heard, quietly left. Nothing makes a record
label more nervous than instability at their distributor.

Lumberjack Distribution was started in 1994 on the model of Mordam.
The idea was to provide the same service for record labels in the East Coast.

Dirk: Lumberjack was at that point trying to be an aggregator of small labels
making sure they got paid but using bigger distributors. So they still used Caroline and Dutch East and all these other distributors. But they wanted the
power of a bunch of labels. It was exactly what Mordam did. They got the idea

from Mordam. They actually consulted with Mordam. You have the leverage to get paid. With Doghouse we never got paid, by anybody. It was always the way it was. We had to sue most distributors to get paid. (Interview no. 18, with Doghouse Records)

Lumberjack was sold in 1997 to Dirk Hemsath, ex-singer for the straightedge band Majority of One and now owner of Doghouse Records in Toledo, Ohio. This is where the search for a buyer for Mordam ended. Soon Ruth was on the phone to her distributed labels to break the news of a merger between Lumberjack and Mordam. New labels had continually been added in recent years, in part as an attempt to recover from the loss of the Green Day and Dead Kennedys sales. But the Mordam contract allows labels to end the relationship at will. Ruth carefully explained that she was not selling the labels to Lumberjack. They were free to leave.[16]

There was a convention of the old and the new held in Las Vegas in January 2005. Some people already had decided to opt out and came mainly to say goodbye to Ruth. In spite of professional presentations and an open bar in Las Vegas, about a third of the labels on the roster soon left. Among the issues were that Doghouse Records has a contractual relationship with WEA, a major label. Some larger labels also felt that they were competing with Doghouse Records. The new Lumberjack Mordam Music Group seemed to be quite different from Mordam operated by Ruth Schwartz. It was not an easy decision to take. Leaving a distributor means that your records in the system get returned to you and the financial burden could easily set a small label back a year. With so many record labels looking around it was not easy to find a new distributor. One of the biggest labels on Mordam, Jade Tree signed a deal with Touch & Go (which is in turn distributed by ADA). Many of the others ended up with Redeye Distribution in North Carolina, as did a Mordam employee, Kristin Attaway. For them it was a good choice. Redeye is efficient and not affiliated with a major label. It regularly wins awards for best small record distributor in the United States. But signing with Redeye would certainly increase the degree of professionalism to beyond what Mordam had ever required.

In the 1980s people in the scene often ordered records directly through the mail.

Kerry: People just don't mail order any more. It stopped in the early 1990s when really good distros started popping up. Blacklist was when it stopped. You didn't have to mail order every band individually. All the hard work that DIY punk has done in the past ten years has made people really lazy. When I was getting into punk I had to buy Maximumrocknroll and read ads and write letters and put a stamp on an envelope and order something because it might be cool. That's how I got my records. (Interview no. 10, with Sin Fronteras)

Blacklist mail order started up with funding from *Maximumrocknroll*. It was the first of distributors that did mail order for individuals that was not tied to a record label. Stephe Perry of Equalizing Distort in Toronto says that "It was significant in that it allowed individuals to buy many titles with one order. I also think it impacted local scenes in that kids started doing distros at shows."[17] Following a struggle by Ebullition, the mail order was treated as a wholesaler by Mordam. Previously it was charged the same prices as a retail store. The extra discount allowed Blacklist to sell these records at competitive prices. The Blacklist collective eventually collapsed but the service was continued by Vacuum Distribution. Other individual mail order services include Very Distribution in Philadelphia and Interpunk.com which accepts records and CDs from small labels on consignment.

Many small record labels are also distributors. Among these are Sound Idea (Burrito Records) in Florida, Hardcore Holocaust in Austin, Texas and Subterranean in San Francisco. Revelation Records in Huntington Beach operates Rev Distribution and Dischord Records in Washington helps out local labels with Dischord Direct. Among such distributors, No Idea in Florida and Ebullition in California have grown to play a key role for DIY punk labels. No Idea is more closely associated with 1990s melodic punk, whereas Ebullition played a key role in the "emo / politically correct" straightedge scene.[18] Through the 1990s, Ebullition had an increasingly important role within the DIY punk scene. Sometimes Ebullition would take 20 copies of a 7" record. But in recent years it has often been 300 or 400 out of a total pressing of a thousand copies. As the distribution grew in the 1990s and 2000s it would also sometimes help labels that had no cash by paying a bill at the pressing plant. This was sometimes done for records that were not available but for which there was a strong demand. Ebullition is still a small DIY operation run by two or three people. It will likely never be more than that. The position that it occupies allows Kent McClard to be independent and also to be independent minded. From a DIY perspective he is sharply critical of the effects of Mordam.

> Mordam to me. . . . I like a lot of people that work at Mordam and I have a lot of respect for Mordam. But at the same time Mordam is a parasite. They don't help anyone except their exclusive labels. They never lifted a finger for me ever in my life. [. . .] They just sit on top and they're parasitic. They just wait for something to get profitable. Then they come and latch onto it. Again, I like a lot

of people who work there. Karin from Spitboy, for example. I've known her forever. But Mordam itself . . . they don't help anyone in this community. They're not participating. They're just sitting on top sucking the best stuff up once it gets big. They were never interested in helping me. [. . .] Once the labels got bigger they would take them away from me. At one point a couple of years ago Mordam sent a letter to every single label we distribute asking them to switch. She [Ruth Schwartz] knew about that. That's not community. I would never, ever approach a label on somebody else's distribution and ask them to switch. That's just vile. I've bought stuff from Mordam for 15 years and she [Ruth Schwartz] does that? That's just insulting! I don't consider Mordam part of my community because they've never done anything for me. (Interview no. 43, with Kent McClard)

The fundamental issue here is not simply that the two distributors are objectively in competition with each other. This is actually the cut-off point between distribution for commercial punk labels and DIY labels as they developed through the 1990s. Bob Suren at Sound Idea mail order makes the same point.

Before Sound Pollution was distributed by Lumberjack/Mordam, every time he had a new record he'd call me up. Every time Sound Pollution did something I'd take as many as I could. I'd take 50. Sometimes 75. I used to buy Assück records from him 75 or a hundred at a time. Once they got picked up by Mordam, Mordam got most of those sales. Now I don't even carry every Sound Pollution title anymore. I was buying them from Mordam. But instead of buying 50 copies I was only buying two or three. . . . Before Six Weeks went to Mordam I used to take 50 or a hundred. Now most of their releases I don't even carry. (Interview no. 34, with Burrito Records / Sound Idea)

Mordam stands at the point where the bigger, more professional labels begin. Mordam can lead to sales to the major label distributors, access to the chain record stores and more. Ebullition guards the line where the DIY labels begin. The people at Ebullition are dispatching records to independent stores and box distributors at punk rock shows throughout the United States and Europe. They are two different worlds. This is the line between the two sectors: commercial labels and DIY punk.

Notes

1. Joe Carducci, *Rock and the Pop Narcotic* (Chicago: Redoubt Press, 1990), 43.
2. Interview with Systematic, *Maximumrocknroll* no. 16, August 1984, 3 pages. This is part of a debate on record distribution that started with a letter from Affirmation Records in the previous issue and continued into MRR no. 17, September

1984 and no.19, November 1984. The issues included a walk-out by some of Rough Trade's employees in San Francisco to protest unilateral decisions imposed from the Rough Trade office in London. MRR temporarily suspended using Rough Trade as a distributor for the magazine as an act of support for the workers. Ruth Schwartz resigned from her job at Rough Trade and soon started Mordam Records. Jeff Nelson reported that Dischord sells to about 40 stores direct but this is only 20 percent of sales. Another 5 percent are individual mail order and 75 percent of Dischord's sales are to distributors. Nelson says that Dischord would like to get involved with an independent distribution network. Available online at www.operationphoenix.com (24 April 2007).

3. John Wilen, "Internet killed the record store?" *Philly Burbs*, 9 March 2007, online at www.almightyretail.com (17 May 2007).

4. Major-label distribution companies that deal in punk records sometimes try to hide their actual status. Some claim that they are "independent" because their offices are in a different building than the major label. Others say they are "indie distributors" meaning that they mostly distribute records for independently-owned record labels and not for the major label itself. The major label has its own branch distribution network that is set up to deal with high volumes of best-selling CDs produced by itself and its imprints. As in other sectors of the culture industries, the effect is to disguise the reality that so much of the business is controlled by a small number of huge corporations. The term for this is an oligopoly.

5. Darren Walters, Interview with Mordam Records, in *We Owe You Nothing: Punk Planet: The Collected Interviews*, ed. Daniel Sinker (New York: Akashic Books, 2001), 110-11. For an earlier interview with some comments on working at Rough Trade see "Ruth Schwartz," in *Threat By Example*, ed. Martin Sprouse (San Francisco: Pressure Drop, 1990), 20–23. There is also an interview with Ruth Schwartz in the special issue on Punks Over 30 of *Maximumrocknroll* no. 110, July 1992, 2 pages. She expresses her distance from the punk community and hopes mainly to operate an ethical business.

6. Mordam Records was also a record label and had a commercial success with an album by the San Francisco experimental metal band Faith No More, *We Care A Lot*, first released in 1985. Mordam Records issued two classic punk records by the Rhythm Pigs, who wrote an anti-*Maximumrocknroll* song for their second album. The band had been criticized by MRR for playing a large commercial concert.

7. I started to do a record distro about 1995 at shows in Toronto that soon turned into Who's Emma infoshop and record store. At the time few kids doing distros at shows were buying from Mordam even though there was no minimum order and the box of records was sent C.O.D. via UPS.

8. Doug Henwood, *After the New Economy* (New York: The New Press, 2003), 66.

9. Editorial note in *Maximumrocknroll* no. 116, January 1993, inside cover. Beginning with the next issue MRR expanded from 144 to 176 pages, lowered some ads rates and began an experiment with free distribution of the zine in San Francisco and Berkeley.

10. The issue of Jeff Bale and *Hit List* is from interview no. 41, with TKO Records, and interview no. 46, with Asian Man. *Hit List* later turned into *AMP Magazine*. For Jello Biafra's differences with Tim Yohannan see "Jello Biafra," in *We Owe You Nothing*, ed. Daniel Sinker, 43–44; and at the Alternative Tentacles website www.alternative tentacles.com/politics (15 October 2006).

11. George Matiasz, e-mail to author, 24 June 2007. See also his column, Lefty Hooligan, "What's Left," *Maximumrocknroll* no. 276, May 2006, 2 pages.

12. "They had schedules and different meetings and groups. It was definitely organized. The whole group and then they'd all split up into different classes and rotate. About digital downloads, contracts, whatever matters were important that year. You went to all of them. Twenty or thirty people and you kinda just sat around. The facilitator would be a person who worked at Mordam. Then everybody put in their concerns or made their comments. The one that I remember was about contracts and how important that was. That's the one I definitely remember." Interview no. 37, with Three One G.

13. Ben Myers, *Green Day: American Idiots and the New Punk Explosion* (New York: Disinformation, 2006), 94.

14. For the effects of the dot-com rush on the city see Rebecca Solnot and Susan Schwartzenberg, *Hollow City: The Siege of San Francisco and the Crisis of American Urbanism* (London and New York: Verso, 2000).

15. Amy Paris, "Bring the Noise," *Sacramento News and Review*, 8 March 2001, online at www.newsreview.com (19 February 2007). TKO Records was with Mordam from 1999 to 2004 but left because the distributor had taken on so many new labels that Mark Rainey felt he was not getting the attention his label needed. (Interview no. 41, with TKO Records)

16. On Lumberjack see Rama Mayo, "Lumberjack Distribution: The Big Takeover," *Punk Planet* 20, September–October 1997, 51–53. *Maximumrocknroll* did not comment on the sale of Mordam distribution. *Punk Planet* carried a fairly neutral report by Kyle Ryan, "Mega Merger in the Indie World," *Punk Planet* no. 66, March–April 2005, online at www.cmykyle.com (19 February 2007). There is a more critical assessment of the merger, IndieHQ, "Lumberjack Mordam Music Group 1 Year Later," online http://indiehq.com (15 August 2006).

17. Stephe Perry, letter to author, 7 June 2007. Information about Mordam is from interview no. 43, with Ebullition.

18. This somewhat objectionable description is from Ross Haenfler, *Straight Edge: Hardcore Punk, Clean-Living Youth, and Social Change* (New Brunswick, NJ: Rutgers University Press, 2006), 14–16.

CHAPTER FOUR

Punk Record Labels
and Social Class

It is a frequent topic in fanzines that individualistic punks are conformists to some musical sound, some look or idea. For the sociologist Pierre Bourdieu this is no contradiction. His term for this is the *habitus* and it expresses the relation between an individual and society. The theme of individuality is important in punk because many participants in the scene are at a stage in their lives where they are becoming more autonomous from their parents. The kind of family from which one comes is still significant. It may be possible in the United States for a teenager to get a part-time job and save up for an electric guitar or a drum kit, but young punk bands still need *some* parent's garage or basement for practice space.

The record-label owners and managers interviewed for this book are not teenagers. They are all over twenty and many are over thirty years. Some are considerably older than that. They may be an unusual group of people: those who stuck it out in punk rock and made it their life. Many of them played in bands and all took on an active role in the scene. They are not kids who passively went to punk shows. So the information given in this chapter may only be valid for this group of people and not for punks who simply went to shows in their teenage years and then moved on with their lives.

This chapter and the one that follows are based on interviews with a sample of 61 record labels that currently operate (or recently ceased operating) mainly in the United States, but including four labels in Spain and four in Canada. It makes no sense to attempt to construct a random sample of punk record labels because this leaves open the questions of the population from

47

Table 4.1.   Age of
***Heartattack* Readers**

Years	Percent
1–15	4%
16–17	15%
18–20	45%
21–23	20%
24–26	12%
27–29	3.3%
30+	0.7%

Source: *Heartattack*, no. 9, February 1996, 32. The zine published 10,000 copies and 285 people responded to the reader poll. This general age distribution is confirmed by other polls.

which it would be drawn. There is no agreed upon list of punk labels. Such a method might also by random chance leave out important labels that have shaped the field and should be included. It makes little sense to write about punk in the United States and not include Dischord and Alternative Tentacles. In such situations sociologists speak about a "purposive sample" but more needs to be said. Sometimes this term simply means the people who could be found and agreed to participate. The record labels interviewed for this book were selected to reflect the diversity of labels in the field as a whole. The sample therefore includes labels that have existed for two decades and some that are quite new. Big labels and small. Famous labels and ones that are almost unknown. A few metal and indie-rock labels that are interested in punk are also included. An attempt was made to have labels from the main centers of punk activity in the United States: Albany, Long Island, New Jersey, Philadelphia, Pittsburgh, Baltimore, Washington, DC, Florida, Austin, San Diego, Los Angeles, San Francisco, Portland, Minneapolis, Chicago, and Ohio.

Each punk generation seems to last for about four or five years. The experience of those who got involved with the first wave of punk in 1977 is different from that of younger participants who discovered punk about 1985 or got involved after 1990. People like Steve Tupper at Subterranean had to hear about punk through the mass media and through record stores. The underground hardcore scene didn't exist in 1977. Punk was a confused mix of bands and ideas that was diffused at least in part by the media. Steve Tupper was alerted that something was going on through the radio.

At that point you had the last of the free-form FM stations still going here in San Francisco. It was called KSAN. There were basically two DJs on that station. KSAN came out of an earlier station called KMPX which was the first ever free-form FM station in the world. They started about 1967 and after a short period they moved over to KSAN and took it over. So there were these two DJs. One was this guy called Richard Gossett who did the evening show. There was this other guy who did the morning shows. The drive-time morning show. They started playing this insane stuff that you couldn't hear anywhere else. It was a commercial station but one of the last free-form stations. They played just about anything that was around. I remember this one actual instance listening to that evening show. The Residents had just walked into the station. Here's our new tape. Put it on the air without even listening to it. Couldn't happen these days. It was the *Duck Stab* EP and it got played immediately. That was the kind of thing they would do. That guy on the morning show played a lot of the Ramones. Richard on the evening show would play just about anything. (Interview no. 47, with Subterranean)

Independent record stores sold some of the records that you heard on the radio. Even the Tower store soon had a small punk section. The local free newspaper would have an occasional article on punk bands. It actually took Tupper a few months to make the link between all of this and interesting looking band posters that were appearing all over the place.

For the next generation things were different. When the media explosion of 1977 punk subsided the scene was more underground. Almost everybody interviewed tells a story about another person who introduced them to punk music. It was sometimes an older bother or sister. Often it was a friend or acquaintance at school who gave them a mixed tape or brought them to a record store. Shy punk kids would sometimes slip a mixed tape into a school friend's jacket pocket. When skateboarding and punk rock were no longer separate scenes, skating was often an important point of access. There were articles on bands in skater magazines but often what was more important were the tapes that other kids brought to play while practicing their moves. What is that music? The 1980s hardcore scene was created through person to person communication at a grassroots level.

Kerry: When I was in highschool somebody gave me a cassette tape. This was the early '80s. I was into Metallica, Slayer and all the good metal bands. And somebody gave me a cassette tape that had D.O.A., Kraut and the Dead Kennedys on it. Two weeks later I gave away all my metal records. It was all Black Flag. The energy. The genuine feeling about it. I saw metal being very thought out and very deliberate about exactly what they were doing. Whereas

I found punk confused, angry, aggressive, questioning, even threatening. I loved it. It was a friend from school. (Interview no. 10, with Sin Fronteras)

Chris: When I was fifteen I knew these two punk rockers. I moved into this area called Clifton. And I ran into these guys and they're, we're going to see these bands play. Sacred Denial. Malignant Tumor. All these little punk bands of the day. So I went with them. It was like this welfare hotel with this dance hall. And all these bands played. That was about 1980 or mid-eighties. I just went there and saw a lot of punk. I was also into Iron Maiden and things like that. I've seen a lot of bands. All kinds of bands. But I didn't go to New York to see something until later, '87 or '88. It started at CBGB's but every Sunday there were shows. In Brooklyn. Or the Ritz back then had hardcore shows. Every Sunday there were twenty hardcore bands playing. (Interview no. 26, with Faction Zero)

Bob: To start with I was in a small town in Florida in the early eighties and about '83, the apex of American hardcore, is when I started getting into things. From then things started to decline. I got into it through my sister's boyfriend who was a few years older than me and he gave me a cassette tape with a whole bunch of really cool bands on it. Hey check out this stuff. I was listening to Black Sabbath or AC/DC. Check this out. There was no track listings on it so I had no idea who the bands were. But I was listening to it everyday and I loved it. Little by little I started noticing people that looked like punk rockers and we started talking and they started telling me who the bands were. I'd play the tape and they'd go, oh that's the Dead Kennedys. Okay if I ever see a Dead Kennedys's record I'm buying it. Flipper. Okay, I'll remember that. Little by little the pieces started to come together. Zines. Records. Going to people's houses and taping a record. Whenever I could get my hands on a zine I'd read it cover to cover. My parents were really flabbergasted that I was getting letters from all over. A letter would show up from Belgium or Holland. Is this for you? Well, who do you know in Italy? (Interview no. 34, with Burrito Records / Sound Idea)

Mark: When I was twelve or thirteen I was interested in skateboarding. In the mid-eighties they went together. Just going to the skater shop with the ramp out the back. And most of the older guys were into punk. The guy who ran it was into punk. The town I lived in had a really great college radio station called WTJU. A lot of punk kids from DC were going to school at the University of Virginia and they had radio shows. In seventh or eight grade I was exposed to these people who really knew their shit. I would just stay up late at night and just tape these shows. When I went to highschool, beyond listening to music, there was a scene, a social scene. (Interview no. 41, with TKO Records)

Yannick: I was extremely young. At school the guy who had his locker under mine was into international hardcore. The harshest you could find. He would surprisingly start taking me to shows. Handing me tapes and records. Brought me to record stores. From early on I was very into record collecting. Going to shows. I would get *Maximum* the second week of the month. Within hours I had twenty letters all addressed to various labels. I'd circle in *Maximum* what I wanted. Whatever I could afford. (Interview no. 51, with Feral Ward)

The underground hardcore scene of the 1980s was created mainly through interpersonal communication and not through mass media exposure. Bands that move to bigger labels with the excuse that they are helping to get the word out are completely mistaken. This is no surprise for social science because communication research repeatedly shows that the main effect of mass media is to reinforce attitudes and beliefs that already exist. Social change and fundamental change at a personal level come through small-group interactions. Having someone make you a mixed tape, bring you to your first show and then interacting with people in the hardcore scene could change your life. Watching a band on television does not have this kind of effect.

But will your parents let you go? In spite of the rebellious image of hardcore punk, the answer to this question is surprising. In academic theories about youth subcultures it is generally held that subcultures involve "resistance" to the adult world. There is much woeful lament in the academic literature about the commodification of subcultures and the incorporation of youthful rebellion by the mass media. It is either turned into images of deviance or youthful fashions.[1] Notwithstanding the negative media coverage of Black Flag and other bands in the early 1980s, and the marketing of subcultures by Hot Topic stores today, this argument rests on a fundamental misunderstanding. The overwhelming majority of people interviewed for this book report that their parents *supported* their interest in hardcore punk.[2]

Iñaki: No. Not at all. My parents separated many years ago and I lived here in Madrid with my mother and my brothers. My father went to Bilbao in the North. There was never any problem. The only thing ever was when about 1990, 1991, 1992, when I started to distribute discs and we lived in a small place and I had my home filled with discs. That was the only problem I ever had with my mother. There's no room for any more! My mother always, she was even interested because I was always at home doing all these things and she would ask why and I would explain. I never had any problem. Never. I never had any problem with my parents, well I'm speaking of my mother because I lived with her, because I wasn't the kind of kid to go out and get drunk all the time. I had problems with my mother, like everyone does. But she never

cared whether I had long hair or short hair or whether I dressed in this way or
that. She saw I was happy doing these things. There was never any problem.
(Interview no. 1, with La Idea)

Jonah: My parents were all right with it. My Mom actually was a sociology, media teacher and she was interested in the lyrics. She didn't like me coming in
late from shows. Walking home. Missing the last bus. But they didn't have a
problem with the music. Any trouble I'd cause they wouldn't blame it on that.
They're smarter than that. (Interview no. 6, with Fuck the Bullshit Records)

Steve: I remember at first they weren't as accepting to it. I was late coming
home from a show. They didn't blame it on the music but at first they didn't
understand it. They were used to what they were into. And then you start
dressing differently. But now they like it and they understand it. They've been
to some shows. They know its not a phase in this point in my life. (Interview
no. 6, with Fuck the Bullshit Records)

Kerry: My Mum wasn't so into it. One day she grabbed me by my mohawk and
cut it off. Now she's vegetarian, very open-minded, a changed lady. (Interview
no. 10, with Sin Fronteras Records)

Johnny Hero: I just live with my Mom. She wasn't crazy about it but so long as
they don't mess up the house. I tell bands that I live with my Mom and you
have to be respectful. You can't get drunk. I had the River City Band staying
and I came down and my mom was having coffee with the trombone player and
talking about fifties rock'n'roll. She got into it too. She kinda liked it. I never
got into dressing punk. This is about as punk as I get. I don't have any tattoos
or piercings or anything like that. Every now and again I get the, you could go
to college still. Student loans. She wants me to give this up a bit and go to
school. (Interview no. 14, with Poor Boy Records)

Ryan: My parents were actually cool. But my brothers were the problem. I
come from a football family. My brothers were two huge football players. I remember the first time I dyed my hair blue and my brother, he kicked the shit
out of me. (Interview no. 17, with Punks Before Profits)

Darren: My parents? I think they were a little freaked out. But I wasn't getting
arrested. I didn't change. My haircut got a little crazy or my clothes got weirder.
But I didn't act that different towards them or towards school. I was always a
bit of a slacker person. That's what appealed to me about punk. I already was a
freak. I got beat up in school. Now I had a reason to get beat up. At least I
looked like a freak. It was all about rebellion, sometimes rebellion just for the
sake of rebellion. Fuck you we look different. We like different music. (Interview no. 19, with Jade Tree)

Jeanine: My Mom liked it. She thought it was pretty cool. She was into Ska. She would listen to the Mighty Mighty Bosstones record. And actually, I feel bad about it to this day, there was this show at Ceecees and there was this band playing. And I was too cool to go to a show with my Mom. So she sat out in the parking lot and listened to the band. I still feel really bad about it. But she was really into it and supportive. Actually, my parents go to every show that Prison Jazz puts together and if the Swims are playing they are always there. They're really into it. (Interview no. 20, with Prison Jazz)

Steve: When I became a straightedge kid my parents were glad. Because before I was pretty wild. Then somehow I got into straightedge. Even though I was getting tattooed and shaved my head, the fact that I didn't drink or do drugs anymore. But when I joined the Krishna they took it pretty hard. They didn't know what that was. It's a cult. But they were cool. (Interview no. 21, with Equal Vision)

Dave: My parents have always been supportive of everything I've done. Once I showed them what it was that I was getting involved with. When I first started booking shows it was at my parents' church. So they'd be there and help out. My Mom would be, this crazy young music! My Dad is a minister. Though personally I don't believe in God, he is a minister. He would be there during the show. (Interview no. 25, with Iron Pier Records)

Chris: I grew up here in New Jersey. New York is a half hour bus ride. My Mom encouraged me to play instruments and play in a band. She would drive me and my band members to play places when I wasn't old enough to drive. She was always about self-expression. She wouldn't have cared if I came home with a purple mohawk or something. She cared about my friends. She cared that I stay out of trouble. (Interview no. 26, with Faction Zero)

Josh: My parents loved it. The bands would sleep over. They'd go upstairs to go to the bathroom or something and hang out with my Mom or my Dad. My parents were awesome. They were really supportive of everything, you know. My dad would come down and watch a band or something. (Interview no. 27, with Trustkill)

Kate: I think they still think it's a phase. No. I think because my brother and I were both always involved at different levels, they don't think that its really weird. They kinda think that everyone our age is into the punk scene! My Mom is definitely, when are you going to stop dying your hair? You're 34 years old. But now I think she is finally over it. There was a while that she was okay, you're going on tour but then you're going to go back to school, right? My Dad was always, I don't care what you do as long as you're happy. Because he came from this business world and he retired early. And he was, I definitely don't want you to do that. (Interview no. 28, with Chunksaah)

Sean: My parents were very, kinda let me do what I wanted. The first time I went to a show I was twelve. I think they dropped me off. My Mom's afraid of driving so it must have been my Dad. Or somehow I'd just take a bus down. I was able to do whatever I wanted. Occasionally a record would give them concern. But they pretty much let me do whatever I wanted. My parents are fairly conservative Catholics. A record cover with blood all over it kinda scared them. But nothing was going to stop me really. When I was twelve either my parents or my friend's parents, they dropped us off at the Chameleon, which was the club, and picked us up. I guess its kinda rare for kids to get into hardcore that young. (Interview no. 29, with Youngblood)

Mike: As far as the music goes my parents were like, oh this is just noise. How do you listen to that sort of stuff. They're into the Beatles and Beach Boys and that sort of thing. This is loud obnoxious noise. But they've always been, I've been lucky, my parents were always very supportive. I think up until maybe four or five years ago, I'm thirty now, up until four or five years ago they thought that it would be something that I would grow out of and eventually get an office job. And do that sort of thing. They realize now that its not just a teenage thing for me. Now they're interested in what I say. You know, my band is going to England in October. (Interview no. 30, with Firestarter Records)

Var: My parents always really encouraged it. They had parameters but the parameters slowly expanded. I did have to leave shows early a lot. Shows used to be a lot earlier back then. They slowly drifted to being later and later. They were always really supportive. My Mom's attitude was get funny haircuts, don't do drugs. They offered me a lot of outlets, a lot of freedom and a lot of support. Because they knew that certain things were natural and were okay and other things weren't. And if you can encourage the things that are okay your kid will never get into the bad things. And I never did. (Interview no. 32, with No Idea)

Kent: There was absolutely no problem. My mother got pregnant in high-school. Her parents didn't want her to go to college. Nobody wanted her to go to college. My Dad split when I was two. I haven't seen my Dad since I was six. She had a few of her own things to deal with. And raised me. There was no. . . . When I started doing shows. . . . My parents have been chaperones for shows that had to have adult supervisors. My parents would come and take money at the door. Perhaps they had some concerns. . . . But they didn't express it to me. I'm sure they thought it was a phase and I'd grow out of it. But they don't care. Not an issue. (Interview no. 43, with Ebullition Records)

Matt: They were pretty lenient with me growing up. I was kind of a wild child. I had a parole officer when I was in fifth grade. One when I was in eight grade. Nothing but trouble. My Mom worked two jobs. So they weren't even home. Later on I wanted a guitar when I was 13, 14. Anything that kept me busy was fine by them. They were really cool. They let us jam in our house. Pissed off the neighbors. They were fine with it. They let me do it. Most of the time they weren't home. But it kept me off the streets. (Interview no. 44, with SAF Records)

Stevo: My Mom was bummed. I remember, it was funny, the first Total Chaos record that came out. Mom saw it. Those guys were the height of punk. And she was mortified. She would not believe it. My Dad was pissed a bit when I told him I was vegetarian. I think he actually said, don't do this to me! My Mom now is much more understanding. She let me get my senior pictures taken with my mohawk and everything like that. I got into *Profane Existence*. A small town. I lived in Band, Oregon. Its funny, they have shows there now. Tours stop there. (Interview no. 48, with 1-2-3-4 Go!)

Gary: My parents were extremely supportive. I was very lucky that way. I wasn't really going out late until I was sixteen. I wasn't allowed to go to a concert until that, pretty much. Like all of a sudden I was allowed to do all this stuff. I think they recognized that. . . . They were hippy skydivers so they were part of an underground thing back in the seventies. They kind of appreciated it in a way. (Interview no. 50, with Accident Prone Records)

Ken: I got involved in the punk scene in Wisconsin in the eighties. Me and a couple of friends in my middle school were the first kids into the Madison punk rock scene. This would have been around 1982. I guess the first show I went to was in '83. I was twelve. My Mom actually took me to shows in the early days. Supportive. Oh yeah. And I was coming home with tattoos at 14. Maybe batted a bit of an eyelid. But they didn't do anything about it! (Interview no. 52, with Dirtnap Records)

Paul: My Mom was really upset with the first mohawk. In 1985, I think. She cried and grounded me. She did understand it was part of this subculture but she also thought it was. . . . She was worried about what her sister, her Mom, would think. It was like an embarrassment to her. (Interview no. 53, with Discourage)

Bob: Initially when I went to see bands like Slayer and Dark Angel in the earlier days before I could drive, my mother and father would take me! They would go and check out the bands too. Because I wanted to go really bad. So they would take me there. And my friend Ron. They would take both of us.

Which was very nice. Very open-minded. My folks were always very open-minded on this. So long as I did good in school it was okay. (Interview no. 56, with Deep Six Records)

Mike: My parents were really supportive. I kinda say they are punks at heart. Neither are into punk but my Mom was part of the feminist movement in the '70s. My Dad was involved in a lot of social justice. They realized it was. . . . Some relatives can't understand it at all. If you don't make money from it people have a hard time understanding it. But my parents realized how healthy it was for me. How much of a creative outlet it was for me. (Interview no. 59, with A Wrench in the Gears)

The most painful examples of problems with parents all have social implications. These include the two American record labels with a strong minority identity: Asian Man and Lengua Armada. And one of the few women at records labels: Pilar at Potencial Hardcore in Spain. Martín Sorrondeguy had serious problems with his father for a number of years because he interpreted punk style as sexual deviance. For a time he refused to walk down the street with his son. Mike Park at Asian Man had to struggle with Korean-American parents who could not accept being a musician as a suitable occupation for their son. (Being a music teacher would have been acceptable.) Pilar in Madrid had to deal with the serious concerns of her mother, who had lived through the repression of the Franco dictatorship, that dressing as a punk would attract the attention of the police. This is not to say that racism and sexism do not exist in the punk scene. Martín insists that they are issues that need attention. However, there are also social reasons for why the hardcore punk scene is generally white, mostly male, and predominantly middle-class. (The scene in the 1980s was also fairly homophobic and even today queer kids are greatly under-represented. One would expect about 20 percent for a scene that is all about being a creative misfit, but the actual responses are about 5 percent and probably many of these are women.)

Are these all middle-class punks? Some actually come from working-class families. What does this mean? Social class is a difficult topic. In the United States it is widely believed that there is no such thing because if you work hard you can achieve anything you want. The truth is that most people move only short distances up or down the occupational scale when compared with their parents' position.[3] The key is to look at occupation and not just income. Bourdieu explains that it is necessary to examine both economic capital and cultural capital. For example, a school teacher earns a fairly low salary but their kids are brought up in an environment that is culturally rich. It is likely they will do well at school and go on to college. In a society where educa-

Table 4.2.   Record Labels and Father's Occupation

Occupational Category	Number in Sample
19. Higher Cultural	5
18. Lower Cultural	2
17. Artists	2
16. Higher Technical	6
15. Lower Technical	9
14. Higher Managerial	12
13. Lower Managerial	5
12. Higher Sales	4
11. Lower Sales	1
10. Clerical	2
9. Skilled Manual	7
8. Semi-Skilled Transport	2
7. Semi-Skilled Manual	2
6. Laborers	1
5. Skilled Service	1
4. Protective Service	0
3. Unskilled Service	0
2. Farmers	0
1. Farm Laborers	0
TOTAL	61

Source: Interviews. Where there are two interviewees the figures in this table represent an average for both. Where the father is absent the mother's occupation is used instead.

tional qualifications are important, parents typically invest money and time in their kid's education. Economic capital and cultural capital are the keys to their children's success.

Those interviewed for this book were asked their parents' occupations. These are ranked according to the scale developed by the American sociologists Richard Peterson and Albert Simkus for their research on musical tastes and social class.[4] The scale takes into account changes in the occupational structure of the United States about 1990, the shift to services and the importance of educational qualifications. It is not a measure of income but of occupational status: economic and cultural capital combined.

Interviews were done with 61 punk record labels (including four in Canada and four in Spain). Because two people were interviewed together at eight of the labels, the sample includes a total of 69 people. It turns out that for most people interviewed their father's occupation is the most significant. In many cases their mother works to supplement the family income. However, eight mothers work as teachers, two as university professors, and there is one lawyer, one architect, one microbiologist and one mother is a stockbroker. In every case these women are married to professional partners. The most usual occupational grouping for the father is higher managerial. The average position on the scale is 13.27 (slightly above lower managerial). Three fathers are doctors, three lawyers, and two university professors. None are policemen, janitors or farmers.

People who do small records labels as a business are part of what Bourdieu calls the new petite bourgeoisie. There is an amount of confusion about what Bourdieu means by this. The term is from his famous book *Distinction* which is based on research done in the 1960s in France.[5] Bourdieu's terms must always be understood in their historical context. The old petite bourgeoisie means craftsmen and shopkeepers: people who run small businesses. The petite bourgeoisie also includes clerical workers and junior executives. Bourdieu noticed that in the 1960s there is a new category of people like journalists, youth leaders, interior designers, therapists and people selling new kinds of craft goods (hand-made candles, jewelry). It was the 1960s! The striking thing about this category of new occupations is that the people who occupy them are very diverse. Some are people who have fallen down the scale from upper-middle class or even aristocratic families in France. Others are working-class kids who are climbing up the scale. Those falling down might be able to use their social contacts and upbringing as interior designers. A working-class kid might be happy to become an activity-leader at a youth club instead of working in a factory. In any case there were fewer factory jobs available. This new petite bourgeoisie in France in the 1960s is basically a diverse bunch of misfits.[6]

Those who run punk record labels today are a different generation. This is not the 1960s. Nor are they the children of what Bourdieu calls the new petite bourgeoisie. Their parents mostly have recognized professions and jobs. They are doctors and business people, airline pilots, geophysicists and microbiologists, electricians and truck mechanics. They are parents who probably hoped for similar careers for their children. Many wanted their kids to go to college. On the other hand, some parents (especially those who were older) had done everything they were supposed to do in the American Dream but did not find it personally very satisfying. Many of these parents grew up in the 1960s and some were affected by its cultural revolution and questioning of the good life. If their kids turned out to be misfits, they might be a little disappointed, but they are not going to force things. The American ideology of the individual runs deep in the culture.

And that is who is mostly doing punk record labels. They are mainly (but not all) dropouts from the middle class. If we take seriously Bourdieu's analysis of the symbolic violence of the dominant culture and the educational system, we might want to say that these are people who have been dropped. Dropped from the team. In many interviews they describe being awkward

Table 4.3.   Level of Education by Record Label

Incomplete high school	1
Finished high school	13
Some college	27
Completed college	14
Graduate education	5
College and law degree	1
TOTAL	61

Source: Interviews. Where there are two interviewees the figure in this table represents their average level of education

and weird kids. Smart kids who had a hard time in school. Kids who went to college often because that was what was expected of them (they came from that *habitus*). A few finished the degree mostly for their parents. Many belong to the category of "some college." Weird kids with huge amounts of energy and creativity were drawn to punk rock.

We should not expect to find such simple relations as working-class kids doing DIY labels and those from the middle-class running more commercial enterprises. If the dynamics of social class were that simple there would be no need for social science. The diagram of the field produced by correspondence analysis shows older labels such as BYO, Dischord, Doghouse, Hopeless, Equal Vision, Fueled By Ramen and Trustkill with many titles released, pressings between 4,000 and 20,000, large number of review copies sent out and best-selling records between 100,000 and 800,000. These are successful older punk labels. And it is worth remembering the large number of record labels that did not continue but stopped after ten or fifteen releases. Looking then at the social field, we find some relation to fathers in higher-technical and artistic occupations. Shawn Stern at BYO is the son of a medical doctor who works as a Hollywood screenwriter. Ian MacKaye's father worked as a journalist and editor at the *Washington Post*. There is also some relation to high levels of education. Josh Grabelle completed law school, but Ian MacKaye did not go to college (though Dischord bands were famous for breaking up because someone left for college).

Below these labels in the field there is a grouping of labels such as Punk Core, Taang!, New Red Archives, Asian Man, Recess, A-F Records, Lovitt, Revelation, No Idea and Jade Tree. These labels are not quite so old, the normal pressings are smaller (2,000 to 4,000), though they have often issued many titles. These are the mid-sized and fairly business-like labels. They may have started off as DIY labels like No Idea and Jade Tree, but they have grown over the years. Looking at the social field, they are some distance from upper-middle class family backgrounds. There is a range from parents in skilled service, semi-skilled manual, clerical, higher sales and lower managerial occupations. In other words, the family backgrounds are working-class to average middle-class. There is a fairly marked tendency for these kids to *finish* school or a college degree. And then they are quite organized and businesslike about how they run their record labels.

The more DIY labels and also new record labels are in the upper left part of the field. They are gathered around the grouping of Fuck the Bullshit, A Wrench in the Gears, Punks Before Profits, Friction, and Grita o Muere (in Spain). These labels have issued the lower numbers of titles, they have the lowest sales, and send out the fewest number of review copies. Looking at the social field they come from working-class families (laborers, semi-skilled transport, lower sales) but sometimes from the middle class (higher managerial). One person did not complete high school. Other sometimes spent a few years at college but without completing a degree. These are the DIY labels done by dropouts.

Figure 4.1 puts at the center of the field two established DIY labels: Lengua Armada and El Lokal (in Spain). These are ideal-typical record labels and a model against which other may be measured.

About half of the people from working-class backgrounds belong to an older generation. They include Nicky Garrett (New Red Archives), Jeff Vanden Berg (Friction Records), Dan Rattown and Felix Havoc. They tend to take their label seriously, along the lines of taking pride on one's job. New Red Archives belongs with the commercial record labels. Havoc Records is a DIY label but operates at quite a large scale. The younger generation of kids from working-class backgrounds such as Craig from Schitzophrenic (in the factory town of Hamilton, Ontario), Ryan from Punks Before Profits and Mike Andriani from Rok Lok have more in common with the drop-out cul-

DIY and new labels with low sales, working and middle-class kids, college dropouts	Old established labels with high sales, often upper-middle class backgrounds or high levels of education
	Fairly business-like labels, working-class or average family backgrounds, tend to complete school or college

Figure 4.1.   The Field of Punk Rock Labels (1990s)

ture of middle-class kids, though this is often accompanied by a strong work ethic. The tension is best expressed by Felix Havoc.

> I was very involved in activism when I was younger with groups like Positive Force and Anti Racist Action. I got very disillusioned with the activist scene in the early '90s. Mostly because I didn't agree with upper-class student types trying to dictate how working-class people should live their lives. I made a conscious decision instead to just work in the hardcore punk scene to support DIY hardcore. My idea is that people will read lyrics and check out bands with relevant social commentary and be inspired to think about issues and form their own opinions. (Interview no. 12, with Felix Havoc)

He doesn't like the idea of people pushing an agenda on others and feels that the existence of DIY hardcore in itself provides an alternative to commercial youth culture. Even if not much more comes from it than loud music and heavy partying.

The question then, is how much trust to put in middle-class dropouts as a force for social change. We are far from the industrial proletariat of classical Marxist theory. Karl Marx was writing about European factory workers in the 1860s. One hundred and fifty years later, what are the prospects for creative middle-class kids who went on tour with their punk bands instead of going back to college? (Over 44 percent have some college education.) Reading Bourdieu on this point is somewhat painful. Because he has absolutely no faith in the new petite bourgeoisie. This is not because of who they are as people, but because of the social position they occupy. Bourdieu argues that struggles for freedom and autonomy require social support. It is difficult for isolated individuals to resist. (During the Second World War the people who resisted the Nazi occupation of France were well integrated into their communities. People who were isolated or lacked social support did what the Germans said.) The new petite bourgeoisie does not have the institutional support of a professional organization. Doctors and lawyers are required to abide by enforceable codes of behavior. This is not the case for many of the new occupations (interior designer, sex therapist). And the new petite bourgeoisie is vulnerable to market forces because it is selling services and luxury goods to clients who tend to have conservative middle-class values.

There is a possible response to Bourdieu and it is based on his own research on university qualifications.[7] His research in France shows that as more people were admitted to the university system in the 1960s, the value of an undergraduate degree declined. Students continue to demand entry to university because for many it is still a good investment. There are also social and personal

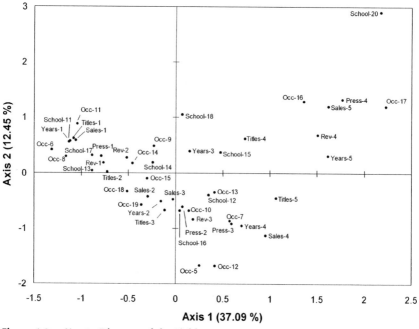

Figure 4.2.   Key to Diagram of the Field
Occ = father's occupation (categories 5 to 19)
School = years of school (11 to 20 years)
Years = years of operation to end of 2006 (1 to 27 years)
Press = normal pressing (500 to 20,000 copies)
Sales = highest sales (1,000 to 800,000 copies)
Rev = number of review copies (1 to 2,000 copies)

	Years	Titles	Press	Sales	Rev
1	1–5	1–15	500–1,000	1,000–2,000	1–10
2	6–10	16–30	1,001–2,000	2,001–10,000	11–100
3	11–15	31–60	2,001–4,000	10,001–25,000	101–400
4	16–20	61–100	4001–20,000	25,001–100,000	401–2,000
5	21–27	101–368		100,001–800,000	

Note: The diagram of the field is based on statistical relations between record labels: years of operation, number of titles, normal pressing, highest sales, number of review copies, and on father's occupation and the persons own years of school. Correspondence analysis produces a diagram of the field in which record labels that are similar are close together and those that are different are far away. The major surprise is that Doghouse and Dischord are placed together. Few people realize the success of Dischord Records over the years, but Doghouse would have been closer to Equal Vision if sales of its bands upstreamed to major labels were included.

reasons for going to college. In this respect, as Bourdieu says, the new petite bourgeoisie is responding to disappointment over the outcome of a college education.

Thus, the new occupations are the natural refuge of all those who have not obtained from the educational system the qualifications that would have enabled them to claim the established positions their original social position promised

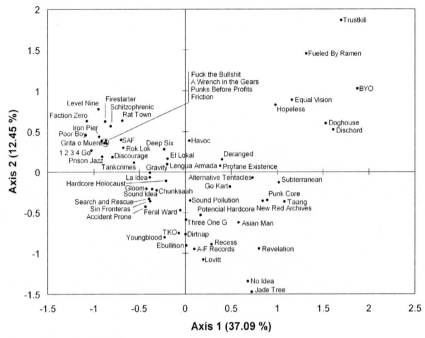

Figure 4.2.   (*continued*)

them; and also of those who have not obtained from their qualifications all
they felt entitled to expect by reference to an earlier state of the relationship
between qualifications and jobs.[8]

University courses in sociology, literature or ecology might be interesting at
a personal level for a year or two. But without the necessary social capital
such a degree is unlikely to result in a high-paying career. Such positions are
increasingly reserved for the students of elite colleges and graduates of pro-
grams in business and law.[9] On the other hand, few people outside the hardcore scene of the 1990s realize the extent to which it provided an informal
education that was different from but perhaps comparable to a year of college. You might even learn how to run a record label.

Unlike other more recognized careers there are few markers of success, especially with a small DIY record label. For some parents it seems as if their kid has
never really grown up. The offices of a small record label often look a lot like a
punk kid's bedroom with boxes of records on the floor and band posters on the
wall. Is this actually a job? Does it have a future? For some parents of kids in
bands there is a moment of recognition when the band starts to tour overseas.
By the second or third tour to Europe or Japan, many American parents start to

sit up and notice. In other cases media coverage is a sign of some achievement. Parents read stories in the newspaper and often clip and save them. At a larger scale, Dirk Hemsath of Doghouse Records found that his father was not that supportive, although his mother provided office space and even sometimes did mail order. It was really not until he bought a warehouse for his record label and distribution business that his father started to recognize what Doghouse Records has accomplished.

Notes

1. The major academic statement on punk subculture is Dick Hebdidge, *Subculture: The Meaning of Style* (London: Methuen, 1979). The book captures something of first generation punk in England but completely fails to understand that it would continue past 1978.

2. Some of those interviewed admitted their parents' support for their interest in punk, for their band, zine or record label in an apologetic way, assuming that their situation was somewhat unique. "I was really lucky with my parents." After thirty or forty interviews in which middle-class parents were almost always described as supportive, the only thing that surprised me was the occasional tale of a parent's strong disapproval. An attempt to develop a scale of family responses mainly shows the generally positive attitudes.

For Greg Ginn's parents' support of Black Flag (Mr. Ginn was a teacher), see Michael Azzerad, *Our Band Could By Your Life: Scenes from the American Indie Underground 1981–1991* (Boston: Little, Brown and Company, 2001), 41–42. And for the Minutemen: "Our folks were working people, my pop was a sailor in the Navy and D. Boon's worked on car radios. We didn't really have resentments against them in the traditional 'kids versus parents' stuff." Mike Watt, *Spiels of a Minuteman* (Montreal: L'Oie de Sravan, 2003), 20. For a later generation of punks see Ronald Thatcher, "Interview with the Parents of the Dead Milkmen," *Maximumrocknroll* no. 30, November 1985, 2 pages. The parents loaned their van so that the band could go on tour.

3. On social mobility in the United States see Doug Henwood, *After the New Economy* (New York: The New Press, 2003), 114–18.

Table 4.4.   Family Responses to Punk Kid

Family Response	Number in Sample
Complete alienation	0
Serious problems later resolved	5
Some concern but supportive	19
Mild concern but generally supportive	17
No problem and active support	20

Source: Interviews. Where there were two interviewees the family response is an average of both. In general they were quite similar.

4. Richard A. Peterson and Albert Simkus, "How Musical Taste Marks Occupational Status Groups," in *Cultivating Differences: Symbolic Boundaries and the Making of Inequality*, ed. Michele Lamont and Marcel Fournier (Chicago: University of Chicago Press, 1992), 152–86.

5. Pierre Bourdieu, *Distinction: A Social Critique of the Judgement of Taste*, trans. Richard Nice (Cambridge: Harvard University Press, 1984), 354–71. For a hilarious novel about the new petite bourgeoisie in Britain in the 1970s and its affinities with first-generation punk rock, see Hanif Kureishi, *The Buddha of Suburbia* (London: Penguin Books, 1990). There is also an interesting account of conflict between German anarcho-punks in the 1980s and the new petite bourgeoisie. See Jane Kramer, "Maxwell (November 1988)," in her *The Politics of Memory: Looking for Germany in the New Germany* (New York: Random House, 1996), 4–49.

6. On the status of professional photographers see Pierre Bourdieu, *Photography: A Middle-brow Art*, trans. Shaun Whiteside (Stanford: Stanford University Press, 1990), 150–73. Martín Sorrondeguy of Lengua Armada and Shawn Scallen of Spectra Sonic Sound (Ottawa) are also serious photographers of the contemporary punk scene. On journalism see Rodney Benson and Erik Neveu eds. *Bourdieu and the Journalistic Field* (Cambridge: Polity, 2005). Sean O'Donnell of Youngblood Records studied journalism, radio and television production and works at the online edition of a local newspaper. Jorge Orsovay at A-F Records has a two-year degree in journalism.

7. Pierre Bourdieu, *Homo Academicus* (Stanford: Stanford University Press, 1988). Attitudes to college among those interviewed are somewhat mixed. Some felt it was a useful experience and helped them to think critically and express ideas. One person enjoyed doing graduate studies in anthropology at an elite university but dropped out because she did not fit in with the social background of other students. Everyone agrees that a university education is not necessary to run a record label. You learn what you need on the job.

8. Bourdieu, *Distinction*, 357.

9. "As more people enter the labour market with graduate qualifications, employers will intensify their screening process by only accepting credentials from elite institutions; those with higher grades; or those with a post-graduate qualification such as an MBA." Philip Brown, "Cultural Capital and Social Exclusion: Some Observations on Recent Trends in Education, Employment, and the Labour Market," in *Education: Culture, Economy, and Society*, ed. A.H. Halsey and others (Oxford and New York: Oxford University Press, 1997), 744.

CHAPTER FIVE

The Dynamics of the Field

Within the punk scene the most usual way to criticize a record label is to say that they only do it for the money. Or that they make decisions about releases with an eye to what might sell. Yet every record label owner says that it has been a hard road and they would not be in this business if they did not love the music. That is what makes it worthwhile. If they wanted only to make money they would have chosen an easier way to do it. The flipside of all this is that old respected punk labels are often forgiven what relations they have with major labels. These are usually indirect and have to do with distribution.[1] Beyond this punks argue endlessly and passionately about the scene. Tim Yohannan is a dictator. *Profane Existence* is politically correct. Six dollars for an LP is a sign that you have crossed over to the dark side. If you are not now, you never were (straightedge). I just love the music. Gilman Street is elitist (by comparison with the Warped Tour). Against Me! are sellouts. And who cares anyhow. Rather than immediately join in these discussions perhaps it is possible to describe the dynamics of the field of punk rock labels.

To understand the dynamics of the field it is first necessary to distinguish the long-established, sometimes famous record labels. These labels have existed for many years, they often enjoy a reputation beyond the punk scene and have an extensive back catalog. These are labels such as Alternative Tentacles (27 years), Subterranean (27 years), Dischord (26 years) and BYO (24 years). These are characterized by a large number of releases, though sometimes there are periods where they slowed up or even suspended activities. They are often closely associated with one or more famous bands. Subterranean issued records

Table 5.1.   Dischord Record Sales

Recording	Total Sales
Minor Threat discography	800,000
Fugazi, 13 Songs	750,000
Fugazi, Repeater	500,000

Source: Interview no. 61, with Dischord Records. Figures are total sales in all formats.

by Flipper. BYO is historically associated with Youth Brigade and 7 Seconds, but had its biggest success with the recent NOFX / Rancid split LP which sold 225,000 copies.[2] Today these are substantial record labels each with an office and perhaps five people working there. Subterranean is mainly a record distributor but still does important reissues of early San Francisco punk bands. Records with a long production cycle and back-catalog sales give most of these labels resources to continue and to issue new records. The most dramatic example of this is Dischord Records.

The remarkable back-catalog sales of Minor Threat are due to the importance of the band and also the integrity of the people involved with it. But made possible also by Dischord's business partnership with Southern Records which handles bulk distribution (previously through Caroline and now through Fontana). Situated in the field of punk labels, Dischord operates differently from SST, which was always more businesslike. And from Alternative Tentacles which is closely associated with Mordam (which also sold Dead Kennedys records through Caroline). These labels are in turn different from Taang! (25 years) which is associated with early Boston hardcore bands,[3] or from New Red Archives (19 years) which is run by the guitarist of the UK Subs. These are among the pioneers of punk and they have survived through many changes. Many other record labels from twenty-five years ago no longer exist.

It is worth noting that back-catalog sales are also an important source of income for major record companies.

Table 5.2.   Current and Catalog Album Sales in the US (in Millions)

Physical Albums	2006	2005
Current	363.9	389.4
Catalog	224.2	229.9
Deep Catalog	158.2	157.5

Source: "2006 U.S. Music Purchases Exceed 1 Billion Sales" www.home.businesswire.com (12 February 2007)

The music industry defines current sales as those within 15 months of release. Deep catalog is older than 36 months. The industry expects more than 40 percent of its dollar revenue to come from back catalog rather than current sales. Back catalog is often sold at a lower price than current hits.[4]

There is another grouping of rather different labels such as Profane Existence (17 years), Sound Pollution (16 years), Havoc (15 years), Lengua Armada (15 years), Deep Six (15 years) and Potencial Hardcore in Spain (20 years), all of which are associated with hardcore music and usually with some kind of radical political commitment. Political hardcore bands. But again these labels must be understood in objective relation to other labels in the field: Doghouse (18 years), Jade Tree (16 years), Equal Vision (15 years), Chunksaah (15 years), Hopeless (13 years), Trustkill (12 years); and No Idea (18 years), Ebullition (16 years), Recess (16 years), Gravity (15 years), Sound Idea (15 years), Rat Town (14 years), and Gloom (12 years). This is a much larger grouping and the labels are quite heterogenous. Some originally came out of the straightedge scene (Doghouse, Equal Vision, Ebullition) but others are associated with more melodic punk bands (No Idea, Chunksaah). Some of these labels seem quite large by punk standards. Hopeless Records routinely has bands with sales between 20,000 and 100,000.[5] Its sister label Sub City and the Take Action tours have raised about $1 million for youth peer-counseling and a Los Angeles youth center. On the other hand, Burrito Records / Sound Idea operates from a small storefront and stubbornly insists on DIY ethics and low record prices. The contemporary field is structured by the relations between such record labels. And this is the field into which much younger participants (Poorboy, A Wrench in the Gears) enter, looking to the older labels and attempting to develop their own strategies.

Within the field as a whole, punk record labels are always started by people with some standing within the scene. It is never simply a business investment. People are in bands, promote shows, publish zines, make videos or at least do a box distribution selling records at shows before they start a record label. From this they have knowledge about bands, about the scene in general, but above all they have social contacts with people in the scene. These contacts are vital.

Kerry: Every single band on my label I've seen live, except for two. I put out 31 records and cassettes over ten years. Later on they were not from Latin America. I was friends of Misery who I saw since 1986. I put out an album of theirs. A band from Seattle. Old friends. I only wanted to put out bands I was friends with. (Interview no. 10, with Sin Fronteras)

Ryan: It's a problem with international bands you don't know. From an e-mail or a hand-written letter they can seem the best person in the world. The coolest. You bring them over to the US to tour and they're complete assholes. Not that this has happened to me but I am very wary of doing bands that I don't know. (Interview no. 17, with Punks Before Profits)

Nate: In the beginning it was very much a regional label. What happened was I did a record for a band called Run For Your Fucking Life, from San Diego, who just played fast hardcore kinda like Poison Idea. They had nobody to put that record out and I had become friends with them and wanted to see it come out. Great record. A friend of mine Matt Average did a band called Reagan SS. He's a good friend of mine. I always wanted to see what he did. I had to put it out because he was my friend. What the label has turned out to be is doing stuff with people I trust and more importantly are my friends. (Interview no. 22, with Gloom Records)

Yannick: On Great American Steak Religion there were Uranus, Drift, One Eyed God Prophesy. Brother bands, for the want of a better term. There was a little triangle between Ottawa, Quebec City and Sherbrooke. Montreal at the time had its own different thing going. I was going to shows pretty much every weekend in those three cities. The bands were friends who would hang out. Those three bands were definitely part of that. Drift were in Quebec City. One Eyed God Prophesy were in Sherbrooke. Uranus in Ottawa. We all just traveled to see each other and hang out. Later on there was Franklin. It was through a friend. And I saw them. One of my best friends was best friends with some of them. It just happened. It felt right. I liked the band. (Interview no. 51, with Feral Ward)

Scotty: Strung Up. Those are some of my closest buddies. That's who I hang with. One of those guys might have been in my garage if we had the meeting there. People who I know through the scene. Just coming up together. Deadfall and Strung Up both started about the same time and we played countless shows together. (Interview no. 60, with Tankcrimes)

Kent: Almost always people you knew. Absolutely. There are some occasions where I would know one guy and he would ask if I would do their record. I did a few, I call them Ebullition by-products. They were one-off things but I wasn't going to keep them in press. Those were things where I didn't have such a connection. I have no interest in doing records with people I don't have some connection with. Its pointless. (Interview no. 43, with Ebullition)

But if you are going to approach a band that you don't personally know, have a good reputation in the scene. Be known for treating bands well.

Table 5.3.   Bestsellers: Bands on DIY Punk Labels

Band and Recording	Sales	Label
Assück, *Anticapital* LP	16,000	Sound Pollution
Aus Rotten, *Fuck Nazi Sympathy 7"*	25,000	Havoc Records
Doom, *Police Bastard 7"*	16,000	Profane Existence Records
Dropkick Murphys, *Curse of a Fallen Soul 7"*	10,000	TKO
DS-13	8,000	Deranged
Engine Down, *Demure*	17,000	Lovitt
Exploding Hearts	20,000	Dirtnap
F.Y.P., *Dance My Dunce*	10,000	Recess
Kagas	22,000	Potencial Hardcore (Spain)
Los Crudos LP	17,000	Lengua Armada
Los Crudos / Spitboy split LP	13,000	Ebullition
Monster X, *To the Positive Youth 7"*	7,500	Gloom
Rapture, *Complete*	9,000	Gravity
Sin Dios first LP	18,000	La Idea (Spain)
Spazz / Lack of Interest 7"	10,000	Deep Six
Swing Kids discography CD	10,000	Three One G
Tragedy LP	20,000	Tragedy / Ebullition
World Burns to Death	7,500	Hardcore Holocaust

Source: Interviews. This table lists the best-selling recording for the label with sales of more than 7,500 copies. Figures include all formats. Los Crudos LP includes foreign pressings authorized by Lengua Armada.

With the success of Nirvana in 1991 and the explosion of Green Day and other bands in 1994, the punk rock scene grew in size. This expanded field changed the conditions for all labels. Shawn Stern has been part of the scene in Southern California from the beginning and observed the changes.

Nirvana definitely helped get the attention of a lot of kids that hadn't listened to punk rock. Granted they grew out of punk rock. But they definitely were a

Table 5.4.   Highest Sales on Mid-Sized Record Labels

Band and Recording	Sales	Label
Anti-Flag, *Mobilize*	70,000	A-F Records
Bouncing Souls, *Maniacal Laughter*	80,000	Chunksaah / BYO
Inside Out	100,000	Revelation
Jets to Brazil	100,000	Jade Tree
Less Than Jake, *Greased*	90,000	No Idea
Less Than Jake	100,000	Asian Man
No Use for a Name, *The Train*	100,000	New Red Archives
V/A, *SF Underground*	75,000	Subterranean

Source: Interviews. The table lists the best-selling recording for the label with sales of over 50,000. The figure for the Bouncing Souls includes 55,000 sales on BYO where it was previously licensed. The Less Than Jake record on Asian Man was later reissued on Fueled By Ramen.

punk rock band when they started. And the success in '94 of Green Day and the Offspring just blew it all open. Every label felt the effects of that. Bands that we were working with were selling 50,000 records. That was unheard of for us. The back catalog. We put everything out on CD that hadn't been out. It definitely got the attention. It died down in the late 1990s. (Interview no. 38, with BYO Records)

Todd: From the mid '90s way up until maybe even last year. I always joked around to whoever was working. Because I have had employees in the past. Next year is our year! Next year is our year. But deep down inside I was like no, its never going to be Recess's year. [. . .] I did have money and gave bands like, $15,000 to record a record. You don't have to do that. Actually sometimes it makes it sound a lot worse. [. . .] We definitely got this trickle down. I think from '95 to '98. [. . .] We were getting trickle down from all that. And F.Y.P. was the biggest selling thing on the label. [. . .] Those were like the gravy days. I had two friends working full time. To me that was a good thing. I was giving them a job and paying them pretty good. Two friends that didn't want to do any other job. I did see some negative aspects that everybody saw, of course. But there was definitely some positive trickle-down things that came because of that. [. . .] I never really wanted to enter that world. Definitely took some of the hand-downs that came from it. Like people who went and got a Green Day record and an F.Y.P. record because of that. (Interview no. 57, with Recess Records)

Bob: I think Green Day and Rancid really spoiled the innocence of the scene. In the 1990s everybody made a lot more money because of all that stuff. When Nirvana and Green Day and Rancid and NOFX and all those bands really blew up, there was a trickle-down effect. Everybody felt it. It happened about the time that Sound Idea was starting up. It went from something that I did on my lunch hour at work and after work to a full-time job in about six months. (Interview no. 34, with Burrito Records / Sound Idea)

This period of expansion in the 1990s helped many long-established labels that were in a position to take advantage of it. New labels were also started in this period. A small number of bands and label owners eventually made substantial amounts of money. But the overall effect was to put the culture of punk under enormous pressure. The accepted practices that developed a decade earlier were often simply set aside. Organizations such as Mordam which provided the infrastructure for that culture were finally transformed into something quite different. Some of this change would have happened in any case. The success of bands like Green Day did not simply spread the word. It put the DIY culture of punk into crisis.[6] Bands that never thought they could have commercial success started to think they could make a lot of money. More cash flowed into the scene. Small record labels expanded and hired more employees. The boom lasted until the end of the 1990s and then labels had to downsize or cease operating.

There have been many markers of the boundaries of punk over the years. Selling 7" records for three dollars. Not having bar codes on CDs. Even not accepting credit cards. These are always contested, sometimes with good reason. One important marker in the field of punk record labels is whether you sign contracts with bands. Mark Rainey sums up the general attitude.

> If the band wants a contract we can do one. I prefer just a handshake deal, which might seem naive. The way I look at it is if I can't trust someone to do a handshake do I really want to be dealing with them anyway? Sometimes with older English bands. Guys that twenty or twenty-five years ago made some very poor business decisions. Hopefully they're not going to be bringing that resentment and directing it at you. It does happen. A lot of times they'll want a contract. I try to keep it as transparent as possible. (Interview no. 41, with TKO Records)

This issue is not as straightforward as it seems. There are often good reasons to make a clear agreement, even for a thousand 7" records. There may not be much practical difference between a friendly e-mail setting out what has been agreed upon over a few drinks, and a one-page contract that the band is asked to initial. But for most record labels having a contract is a significant marker. It means that this is not just friends helping each other but that relations are now on a more business footing.

Table 5.5.   Labels That Have Written Contracts with Bands

A-F Records	Punk Core
Alternative Tentacles	Revelation
BYO	SAF Records
Dirtnap	Search and Rescue
Doghouse	Taang!
Equal Vision	Three One G
Fueled By Ramen	TKO
Hopeless	Truskilll
Jade Tree	Youngblood
New Red Archives	

Source: Interviews. Alternative Tentacles normally does contracts but it is not a requirement. The Youngblood contract is one page. TKO and Dirtnap sometimes do contracts.

Most of these are contracts for three albums, or two albums and an EP, but there is often some flexibility possible. Some labels are now licencing albums for three or five years, especially for reissues of older records. There are different kinds of contracts. Some have been prepared by lawyers and are twelve or fifteen pages long. For sure, an e-mail or a one-page agreement could prevent misunderstandings in the future. The person in the band who looked after these matters may leave. People may not remembers details years later. Some small record labels issue as many as twenty releases in a year. That is a lot of details to remember.

Some labels like Fat Wreck and New Red Archives sign contracts for only one or two albums. This allows the band the freedom to look around for their next album. A written contract really comes into play when another record label wants your band. The status of the recordings already issued on your label is seldom a problem. Even major labels with high-powered lawyers will normally leave previous recordings with the indie label. But what if the band still owes money to the smaller label? More critically, a contract allows a small label to negotiate a buyout. If the contract was for two albums and an EP and there is still one album to go, the smaller label is in a position to negotiate for financial compensation. Perhaps in some unspoken way this is the objection to contracts in the close-knit DIY punk scene. Signing a contract means that the friendship may not last, or may eventually turn into more of a business relationship.

Another issue is whether labels insist on bands touring. Every label likes their bands to tour and especially feels disappointed if a band breaks up and cannot play out to support a record. Firestarter in Baltimore is probably more explicit about this than other DIY labels.

Mike: Minus a few exceptions I always wanted bands that were going to work. Work themselves. Even if it was just a week-long tour on the East Coast. Bands that were going to work. To play shows and stuff. So that was important to me. There were only so many of those bands in the area. (Interview no. 30, with Firestarter Records)

Stevo: I insist on bands touring now. I didn't back then. There have been bands where that's my first question. Are you going to tour? I would expect that a band would at least try to do a national tour a year. Two weeks here and there as well. Let's do a two-week East Coast tour. Or a two-week West Coast tour. Because I love putting out really good music. But it becomes really frustrating when a band says they're going to tour and don't. And the record just stalls. (Interview no. 48, with 1-2-3-4 Go!)

Yannick: Requirement about touring. No. Definitely not. I tell the bands that.
. . . A lot of people wonder why other bands are big and they're living off it.
And I tell them you have to spread the word around yourself. You gotta go play
to people. Bring them your LP. That's how you sell more than the 3,000 quantity that normally. . . . There are less bands touring. The touring circuit has
shrunk. It's not as easy to book a good solid tour anymore. (Interview no. 51,
with Feral Ward)

But there are other bigger labels where touring is required. It is in effect a
condition of being signed to the label.

Dave: If there is one prerequisite its not their hair, its not their clothes, maybe
not even their sound. They have to be hard working, they have to be willing
to tour. We can do a world of things for the band. We can promote them, pub-
licize them, get them distributed. But if the band's not on the road working,
bringing their sound to the world, its like fighting with one hand behind your
back. The ultimate goal for all the bands (not all reach it) is for them to be professional musicians and do this for a living. (Interview no. 24, with Punk Core
Records)

Shawn: We ask them to tour. Because if you don't tour its going to be real difficult to sell records. If you're a band that's a part-time band then I don't care.
I could think you're amazing but the chances of me wanting to spend money
on putting your record out. . . . Who's going to buy your record? We're looking
for people that are trying to earn a living from playing music. Its pretty much
a business and you've got to treat it like that. Touring eight, ten months a year.
It's a full-time job. If you want to earn a living off of playing music it's a full-
time job. (Interview no. 38, with BYO Records)

Nicky: I don't have any requirement that they tour for six months or eight
months. But don't whine at the label if the record doesn't do well. I have one
band, who actually live right around the corner from here. Actually a couple
of the bands took issue with my promotion. They wanted me to spend $1,500
on an ad in some glossy magazine. My answer was well, firstly the kids you're
selling records to don't read these glossy magazines. They read the fanzines.
And secondly, I'll do that when you do a major US tour. Don't come to me asking for things like that if you're not prepared to go out there and sell the record.
(Interview no. 45, with New Red Archives)

Jesse: But there's no requirement. We have plenty of bands that are touring not
at all. Or just a few gigs. Then we have a band like Akimbo who is really slog-
ging it out on the road six to eight months a year. I Object! also is always on the

road. And they do it DIY style. They never ask for anything except CDs or whatever. We love bands like that. (Interview no. 49, with Alternative Tentacles)

Dave Punkcore says that the best way to approach a label is not to send a
demo but to get out there and tour. The label is looking for a band that is
making a name for itself. Mid-sized labels will sometimes accept a band that
can only do limited touring, but in that case they usually put less resources
into the project. Mark Rainey at TKO says that in the Green Day and Offspring boom of the 1990s it was easy to sell 1,000 records. Today he looks for
a band that has funded its own tour and recording. With a reissue of an older
band there is less expectation of much touring. Some labels just want the
band to be honest about what it will do. Bigger labels that invest $25,000 or
$50,000 in a young band certainly expect that it will tour for eight or ten
months a year.

These kinds of issues make the boundaries between DIY and commercial
punk labels. Most DIY punk labels see a difference between what they are doing and a large label like Epitaph and even Fat Wreck Chords. This is the
case even when the person likes some of the bands on the bigger label.

> Martín: Epitaph? At this point that label is more about moving units. I'm sure
> that somebody at that label likes the bands but it seems like the popular bands
> that they know sell. I think that the difference between what I do is that there
> could be a band and I don't give a shit if it's going to sell. I'm into it and I want
> to release it because I'm that into it, because its something that I feel is im-
> portant. . . . Epitaph, they're not a part of my scene. I don't know those people
> individually, personally. But what they do as their work I don't associate with
> it. (Interview no. 5, with Lengua Armada)

> Ryan: The difference between us and Victory? Punk rock and hardcore is my
> life. But with some of their practices they seem different. My friends were in
> Washington and went to look around Dischord House. Ian MacKaye waved to
> them. Hey what's up. Talking with them. But Victory is so corporate, so stained
> with money. They have contracts with bands. Earth Crisis. Contract with Vic-
> tory for three records and if you break up we have rights to your new bands!
> Extreme contracts like that have nothing to do with punk and hardcore. (In-
> terview no. 17, with Punks Before Profits)

> Var: I look at Trustkill and that's something that I'm relatively unfamiliar with.
> I have one of their first 7"s somewhere. But my impression is that this is a la-
> bel that puts a huge emphasis into chain distribution, marketing to the glossy
> over-ground, which has become MTV-land and its so removed from my realm
> of knowledge that its not music I listen to, its not a world that I partake in. It

just doesn't really affect me. If you take that and say Victory, or labels like that, I have no knowledge of that or connection to that. This is like you go to the mall and you watch MTV you know about this music. I'm not slamming it. That has nothing to do with me. Good, bad or indifferent its just a world I don't walk across. I can't tell you anything about the new Victory record. Its worlds removed. (Interview no. 32, with No Idea)

Bob: I wouldn't mind selling 50,000 copies of my records. But I want to sell it my way: on vinyl for a low price through the mail and in cardboard boxes at shows. I don't want to have a bar code on it and have it inside Blockbuster or Best Buy. I open the Sunday paper and Victory Records had a co-op half-page advertisement with Best Buy Records. It was a big Best Buy logo on one side and a big Victory logo on their other side. All the new Victory titles. Get them all at Best Buy for $9.99. I don't want to go that route. (Interview no. 34, with Burrito Records / Sound Idea)

Mike: Victory records? To be honest I cannot relate to anything like that at all. For one the music is not. . . . I'm not into that music. I know that sounds like a generalization but I've never heard a band on Victory that I liked. I'm into hardcore punk. Not that stuff. That scene as a whole is just very machismo and apathetic. Again that's a broad generalization. But I've been to those types of shows off and on and I've only felt hostility. I haven't felt comfortable at all. Those are the vibes. But that whole scene: these are the people I was trying to escape when I got into punk when I was in high school. It's like that kind of infiltration. I find it hostile. [. . .] Being on that level. Contracts. Promotional kits. All that is not what I'm about at all. (Interview no. 59, with A Wrench in the Gears)

Sometimes a small DIY label even makes a distinction between itself and a respected but larger DIY label. Dischord, Alternative Tentacles and BYO have a legendary status for someone just starting out. Even a label like Havoc or Asian Man may seem big.

The general issue of relations between larger and smaller labels is often difficult for interviewees to speak about. It is a small world and you could easily have to deal with someone in the future. There is quite a bit at stake. For example, it is now routine for commercial punk labels to license vinyl editions of their CDs to smaller labels with which they have good relations. For their part, the bigger record labels are sensitive to accusations of poaching bands from smaller ones. Small labels speak in vague terms of not wanting to hold a successful band back. Big labels say that there are so many tiny outfits today that it is practically impossible to come across a band that does not have a 7" record on some obscure label.

This relation of being in objective competition affects labels at all levels. At Doghouse Records the Get Up Kids sold 150,000 records. Dirk Hemsath explains:

> We put out their first EP and we put out their album. And their album to that point had sold maybe 50,000 copies. And obviously for us it was a huge success. And everybody was coming after them: major labels and bigger indies. I remember them talking to Epitaph, of course a lot of majors. So they ended up getting a manager who was also starting Vagrant at the time. They were going to sign to Mojo, which was the label that had the Cherry Pop and Daddies, or something. It was like a swing label, but it was part of a major label. So at the time I was like, well if that's what you want to do. It's an upward move I guess. They still owed us a record, so we were negotiating a buyout for it. And then they kind of switched and decided they were going to sign to Vagrant, which was a start-up label at the time. So it was a little bit of a battle just because Doghouse was bigger. . . . (Interview no. 18, with Doghouse Records)

At that point Vagrant had a couple of compilations out but was not yet operating as a full label. The Get Up Kids were the start to that. Dirk now has a good relationship with Vagrant, but at the time things were rough.

> Louis: There are many different ways an artist can move from one label to another. In the case of Dillinger Four we had signed them for a two-album deal and they did their two albums. We discussed with them about re-signing them and they decided to do a one-off with Fat Wreck Chords. Then at some point after that they went to No Idea. Or maybe No Idea was in the middle, I can't remember. In the case of Thrice they were still under contract to us and so the other label had to come to us and buy us out of that agreement. Each case is different in the way that it is handled. Its bitter-sweet if the artist is moving upward. We love working with them and we'd love to grow with them. But at the same time we understand that there are other companies with more resources. In that case we want to be fairly compensated for doing the heavy lifting, as they call it. (Interview no 42, with Hopeless Records)

At Equal Vision, Steve Reddy explains that the relationship between bigger and smaller labels has changed over the years. There are now many more channels of communication by which bands can become known.

> Chiodos came from Search and Rescue. Sure it happens more. There are just so many labels. I can remember when there were just a handful. Positive Force, Alternative Tentacles, SST. Now there's so many. These kids they're hearing about their friends getting together in high school. I did a label for a friend before

Equal Vision called Combined Effort. And from when we wanted to do it, it took six months of gathering money. Getting information about how to do it. Now that information is easily available. Kids have a lot more money and so it is easier for that stuff to happen. There's more avenues to sell. Back then there was one avenue: you took out an ad in *Maximumrocknroll*. And you just went to your post office everyday to see if you found $3 there. That was it. It was simpler but there weren't so many avenues. (Interview no. 21, with Equal Vision)

Today there are many more small labels that give unknown bands a start. In the early 1980s there were much fewer. And it is no longer a matter of waiting for an interview in *Maximumrocknroll* and attracting interest. Bands now get exposure on the internet through MySpace, PureVolume and through many punk news websites.

The process of a band moving from one label to another involves some negotiation for everyone involved. Bob Shedd takes care of this at Revelation and he describes what is probably a typical example.

In reality we're talking about a smaller independent label to a bigger independent label. What's the difference? Usually it's just catching the attention. Some labels might go in and say, come over here. We'll give you more. For me I don't want to do that. I just say here's what we can offer. I don't want to step on toes but maybe we could work together. And let's make sure that we line up with our goals. Shook Ones, who are a little bit poppier. They were on Endwell Records, a Canadian record label, a great punk hardcore record label. With us it was me approaching them and saying hey, I love your band. I think you're a great live band. And they wanted to work with us. They didn't really have a formal contract with Endwell. They let him know and he was more than happy. And actually when a band like that is brought to a bigger label a lot of times it helps that smaller label. It helps with recognition. We left the earlier recording with the smaller label. Had the label approached us maybe we would have taken it and I believe that has happened in certain cases at Revelation. Sometimes its better for the small label to do that. (Interview no. 40, with Revelation)

In this case the smaller label was happy to see the band picked up by a well-recognized label. To have a band move to Revelation could be a good thing. Bob Shedd says there usually is some connection with a band prior to signing, but he has approached a band cold. "Hey guys, I saw you play and I think you're great." It is a tricky situation. In spite of everyone's tact and goodwill the smaller label is losing a band that could have made a significant contribution to its future growth. Everyone is aware of this. Occasionally the smaller label is allowed to release a future EP or perhaps licence an album for release on vinyl. Even with goodwill on everyone's part, it is objectively a situation of competition between two record labels, which are often operating according to quite different models.

> Gord: I don't have written contracts and I don't want any. But its getting to the point where its getting a bit tricky. But I have no plan on introducing contracts whatsoever. Unless the band is the one that requests it I don't want to. A handshake or an e-mail. And you can keep this e-mail as word of law as far as what you're going to get from me. So I'm trying my best to avoid the whole contract element. A lot of the bands that I've been working with over the years are getting fairly popular now. Bands are always free to come and go. But it does hurt a little bit when you've been working with this band for a long period of time. And for whatever reason they now choose to work with another label. (Interview no. 54, with Deranged Records)

No Idea Records is very outspoken about this issue. The mid-sized label in Gainesville, Florida has had its share of success but still operates within the DIY punk scene. Asked about smaller labels that tactfully say they are pleased with the recognition their labels get and say they don't want to hold a band back, Var Thelin is skeptical. Sometimes the person never had any intention of taking their label beyond simply working with friends. So there is no sense of entitlement.

> I tend to be exactly the opposite. I tend to be incredibly possessive of the bands and the relationships that we have and it means a hell of a lot to me. I won't lie. I won't say its awesome. I'm proud or it validates what I do. I'm not going to lie. . . . I probably would have mortgaged what I could have to put out the next Against Me! record. (Interview no. 32, with No Idea)

No Idea has always had a good relationship with people at Fat Wreck Chords. And Var called them and said, what the fuck have you just done to me? Later that day Fat Mike returned the call and said, let's talk about it. But Fat Wreck still signed Against Me! Somewhat ruefully, Var says at least he got a call from Fat Mike. "Would the guy from Sire have called me back? Probably not, you know." (After releasing two albums on Fat Wreck Chords, the band signed with Sire, a major label.) There have been other situations where a band from No Idea has left and because of the band's personal situation Var agreed it was a good thing.

Most punk bands do not exist in the high-flying world of Against Me! and the small number of bands that have had this kind of commercial success. For a return to reality look at a small label such as Rat Town, in Florida. Dan is well organized but ultimately his record label is a passion rather than a job.

For somebody at my level with the label, I think that the ideal situation with the label would be a band that put out a record would go on to a bigger underground label. I would hate to be involved with any band that went through a major label. Pretty much every band I put out a record for broke up. Every tour for every band I've put out has become a book of horror stories on the road. Bands have broke up on the road. I'm stuck with a box-load of records. It's ironic. It's funny. I'm not mad about it. The music is still there. (Interview no. 31, with Rat Town)

Many punks are record collectors. The traditional punk formats are cassettes and vinyl. Cassettes are popular in parts of the world like Mexico and Latin America where kids do not have access to expensive stereo systems.[7] Trading cassettes was important in the 1980s in the underground punk and metal scenes. The format continued into the 1990s. Fugazi sometimes sold 130,000 cassette copies of an album. But the major punk format is the vinyl record. Pressing plants still operate in the United States, though in some European countries none remain. In recent years a pressing plant in the Czech Republic has been offering high-quality work at good prices. The major challenge facing the music industry and DIY punk labels is digital downloads. Some small labels such as Lengua Armada welcomed "illegal" downloading of their releases in the 1990s. They were unable to keep pressing their records and viewed downloading as similar to an earlier generation of tape trading. Many but not all punk bands take a liberal attitude on this issue. The policies of the Recording Industry Association of America, including prosecuting teenagers for illegal downloading are not widely popular. Besides, many punk musicians download music themselves. Most punk labels (not all) were quick to set up websites in the 1990s and some operate online stores.

Ryan: I don't like the whole iTunes thing. Its too much rush. Its taking the shelf life of records. . . . I read MRR monthly. But I'm going at my pace. I'm not going to put out a record on August 5 and expect everyone to have it August 6 and then by August 20 have it be an old record. If more labels decide not to keep up with this fast-paced world I think we'd see a significant change. (Interview no. 17, with Punks Before Profits)

It took some time to come to grips with digital sales. Punk labels were at first uncertain if their bands wanted their material sold in this format. Especially because many people purchase a single song rather than the full album. How would the new revenue be split between the label and its bands? For many small labels it seemed like a lot of work. But record distributors were soon offering to do most of the technical work, for a fee. By the end of 2006 most punk labels were selling songs and albums digitally. As in the mainstream industry, iTunes accounts for the bulk of sales. Revenue to labels from digital music services grew rapidly in 2005–06 but for most labels it still represents less than 10 percent of their dollar revenue. This is similar to the mainstream music industry where about 10 percent of sales were digital in 2006. There are surprises. Sometimes a band that cannot be sold on CD (there are still boxes of them unsold) does well with digital sales.

> Johnny Hero: CDs are so disposable. You throw the case away and put the CD in your CD wallet in your car and it gets all scratched up and you burn a copy. Now you have a burned copy. Vinyl is forever. I love it. (Interview no. 14, with Poor Boy Records)

> Dan: Around here just recently kids have been raiding their parents' attics and getting record players. Three years ago at a distro I couldn't sell one record and now I'm selling more records than CDs. Couldn't be happier about that because I've been collecting vinyl since I can remember. (Interview no. 31, with Rat Town Records)

The future is anybody's guess. It is likely that in the punk scene there will be a resurgence of vinyl. Record turntables are still being manufactured. Kids are digging around in basements and attics for the stereo systems their parents put into storage when they bought a CD player. A new generation of turntables can turn vinyl into MP3 files. Punks love vinyl and the older generation never accepted the CD format. Vinyl creates problems for major distributors because it is heavier and requires more warehouse space. In the United States an efficient DIY punk distribution system survived the 1990s and is set up to deal with vinyl records. We may even see a demand for reissues of out-of-print records by kids who regard the CD as an inferior and disposable format. Touch & Go Records reissued in 2006 a limited edition vinyl LP of the early 1980s hardcore band the Fix. The purchase of the 12" record entitles the buyer to download the album in MP3 format using a unique password included with the record. This combination of vinyl and MP3 is probably the future of punk rock.

Notes

1. One of the few public criticisms of Dischord comes from Kent McClard. "They use all the most hideous and horrible distributors that there are, their records are way over-priced in stores, they put UPC code stickers and shrink wrap on their CDs, and their records are sold primarily through record stores and hardly ever at shows by kids

doing small distributions." By The Way, Please Fuck Me, column in *Maximumrockn-roll* no. 179, April 1998, 1 page. Dischord Records has an ad in this issue of MRR. At one point Tim Yohannan suggested that Dischord should invest some of its money in an alternative distribution network. But the label obviously felt some personal loyalty to John Loder and Southern Records.

2. About 20,000 of the NOFX / Rancid split were on vinyl. The total sales of 7 Seconds, *Walk Together* are 125,000 and the Youth Brigade records sold 80,000 and 70,000 copies each. Royal Crown Revue did over 50,000. Interview no. 38, with BYO Records.

3. Taang! is usually remembered for classic Boston hardcore such as Gang Green and Jerry's Kids, but also had a college radio hit with the Lemonheads in 1989. The label today licences classic English punk bands for release in the United States. The Lemonheads, *Lick* probably sold 75,000 copies. E-mail to author from Cory Brennan, 12 January 2007.

4. Geoffrey P. Hull, *The Recording Industry*, 2d ed. (New York: Routledge, 2004), 173-74.

5. Hopeless Records biggest success is the second Avenge Sevenfold full-length with US sales currently at 340,000 copies. It will eventually go gold (500,000 sales in the USA). The label has two other band recordings over 100,000 and the Take Action tour compilations sell about 50,000 copies.

6. There is some evidence that the Green Day generation did not explore punk history much beyond Minor Threat and the Dead Kennedys. Throughout the 1990s there was little interest in the Subterranean back catalog. It was only after the boom was over that there started to be some interest in reissues of bands such as Code of Honor. A label like Gravity with bands like Heroin and Antioch Arrow would not have benefitted directly from the Green Day and Offspring explosion but did manage to get better distribution (through Mordam) because of the general expansion of the field in the 1990s.

7. Martín Sorrondeguy points out that much Latin American punk exists only on cassettes. Some of these tapes are disintegrating and unless the music is reissued much of the history of punk in Latin America will be lost. Labels in the USA that have issued Latin American punk include Lengua Armada, Profane Existence, Sound Pollution, Six Weeks, Sound Idea, Catchphraze, and especially Sin Fronteras (on cassette and vinyl).

CONCLUSION

What About the Music?

The challenge for a record label is to have enough of a sound or identity that it functions as a "label" for people looking for new records. But at the same time the actual record label must be open to new bands that are not simply repeating what has already been done. Punk music does not stay still: styles evolve and change. Doing a record label is an activity that unfolds in time. Based on what the person doing it knows, or perhaps on who in the scene they know, decisions have to be taken that involve uncertainty. Will other people like this band? Will it sell enough copies to break even? Does it fit the label? This is one of the most difficult parts of the interview for record labels. They attempt to describe the bands they have released. Sometimes this includes a fairly wide range of musical styles and sounds. Every record label has *some* identity. Punk Core is a label that is tightly associated with a "street punk" look and sound, though Dave Punkcore dislikes the term street punk. Accident Prone is a label that mainly issued records by Gary Bahen's friends in San Diego. This dedication to friends and community is admirable but Gary says it probably limited the label's effectiveness because the range of music is too wide.

Bands think carefully about the effects of being on a certain label. To some extent they become associated with its image and with that of its other bands. Being on a record label adds some layers of meaning. This is the reason why bands want to be on Asian Man Records even though Mike Park insists that he can do nothing for them. This is not quite true. Asian Man has good distribution through Lumberjack Mordam Music Group, but even more important it is Asian Man Records. Having an album on the imprint is a mark of distinction within the scene. A young band that has little influence might have to accept an offer from a label that is not appropriate, but they will attempt as soon as possible to move to a label that better matches their sound or image. Mike Park would probably advise them to do it themselves.

Many DIY labels today come from a successful band. In the years that it is active, most of the other bands on the label are those with which it played or toured. These relations of affinity are musical. A punk show today tends to include bands that are somewhat compatible. But above all these relations are social. As in any performance activity there is a great deal of time spent waiting around. Musicians and music fans have strong common interests. There is a great deal of time to get to know other people. Bonds form on the basis of a shared life world. People talk endlessly about music and gossip about the scene. Everyone on tour is broke. So cheap places to eat, cheap or free diversions (skateboarding, throwing a ball around), and records and t-shirts swapped among bands. The best thing you can ever say about another band is that they are awesome people. You enjoy hanging out with them. A record label that is based on a touring band is built on friendships.

A DIY punk record label is constructed on these kinds of social relations. The decision to sign a band at this level is not an economic calculation. It is certainly not the result of an A&R department making a business decision to invest in a band. Major labels have always hired intermediaries in an attempt to simulate relationships of friendship and trust. Punks who have been part of the DIY scene should be able to tell the difference. At the DIY level, a record label is built on knowing other people, often on significant relationships. This social logic makes the signing of contracts almost completely inappropriate. The relationship is based on friendship not on a legal contract. The ordinary social life of the scene (hanging out, watching other bands, sharing meals) enters into the construction of a record label. It is the mortar that holds it together. This is even more pronounced when the person doing the label acts as a producer in the recording studio, or perhaps does backing vocals or additional guitar on one or two tracks. Being on a label is not an external matter but part of the social and perhaps even the musical development of the band. Many independent bands have already recorded songs before approaching a label, but the encouragement of the label is a factor in writing new songs.

DIY record labels make decisions based on a social logic. This is another version of what Bourdieu calls a *habitus*. It is tacit knowledge based on a social background (family, school) and on experience of the punk scene. This includes a familiarity with punk history and musical styles. And a guess about where these are going in the near future. There is a revival of early 1980s sounds, but you have to be a bit different and not simply repeat the past. The underground sound of emo bands in the 1990s has been completely commercialized and this vein is exhausted. Most record labels and bands understand this. But who knows, some new variant might be possible.

To do a DIY record label is to be involved in this rich texture of musical and social relations. It is little wonder that many people find it both fascinating and fulfilling at a personal level. People with jobs and professional careers continue to run record labels in the evening and on week-ends. Instead of the bands coming over to stuff 7" records and inserts into plastic bags, it is sometimes grandfathers who enjoy helping out. One person jokes that other people at his place of work spend this amount of time and energy on golf! In a way, running a record label is a kind of a game. But as Bourdieu says, many of the games we engage with are also serious matters. People play games with passion and skill.

As in any game or enterprise there is an element of risk in running a record label. There is an economic risk, minimally $1,800 for a thousand 7" records. You may not get that back. Punk record labels and distributors have also faced legal prosecution. (In Germany for a record cover with a Nazi symbol on an English policeman's helmet. This ironic use of the Swastika is not permitted under German law.) But the most usual risk is in putting out a record that falls completely flat. A series of these will affect a label's reputation both with bands and potential record buyers. This is weighed in the balance at the moment when a record label applies to a distributor. There is often a formal application process, not that different from a job application. The label in effect submits a resume to be evaluated.

In some ways the most significant evaluation of the label comes from the scene itself. In interviews when asked about other labels, most people took this as a request for their evaluation. It was often expressed with some tact. He's a really nice person but I don't much like the recent bands he's put out. And often a disclaimer: but maybe that's just me. In complex ways, within the field, people are continually being evaluated by their peers: I really like that label. I don't know where he gets the energy to do so many releases. And every record beautifully produced and with really consistent artwork. But that other label is really diverse. Its hard to know what is behind it. There doesn't seem to be one person guiding it. Its all over the place. This kind of peer evaluation is central to the operation of any field.

The evaluation involves knowledge and skill that is specific to the punk scene: knowledge of bands, musical styles, what is happening now or in the near future. But it also involves general social skills, organizing ability, fairness in dealing with people. The all-important factor of being a really awesome person. These are individual and social skills and Bourdieu insists that family background is crucial, though later experiences in school and in the punk scene would play a role. It is therefore not surprising that people who are drawn to each other may share similar structural positions in the social field. And as we have seen many people involved in record labels are middle-class dropouts. So a scene in the United States and Canada that is more or less based on a shared *habitus*. On similar experiences of mainly middle-class families, some variations in school, on shared experiences of frustration, difficulties in meeting expectations, disappointment with school, family, self. And all this not external to the music but actually what much of hardcore is about. Not only at the level of lyrics but musically: fast, angry, distorted, shouted. And then a social space where these general ideas and emotions can be expressed, recognized by others (often in complex ways, including some misunderstanding) and ultimately rewarded. And this reward, like the invisible stage at punk shows, is nonetheless real for being completely understated. You guys were awesome. Can I get your new record.[1]

But if this is the dominant social logic of hardcore punk it is also challenged. The experience of punks outside the United States and Canada is different, often radically different. And not all those who run punk record labels in the USA come from middle-class backgrounds. There is a solid minority of people from working-class families. Among these some of the older people run DIY labels with considerable energy. A few are responsible for businesses that may employ twenty people. Some of the younger working-class punks are closer to the world view of middle-class dropouts, but with an odd tendency to be a bit more businesslike.

The experience of Latino punks in the USA is now a real challenge to a scene dominated by white middle-class kids. In complex ways, sounds from peripheral parts of the world (Scandinavia, Brazil, Quebec, Japan) challenge and revitalize American hardcore music. Slowly, women in punk and women in bands are having an effect on the field as a whole. Much of this challenge comes from the margins. Many women's bands in the 1990s were not on DIY punk labels (Spitboy was a notable exception) but challenged the scene from slightly outside its boundaries.[2] This is also true for queer punk. The queercore movement of the 1990s existed at the margins of DIY punk. Few people in the scene liked Pansy Division's sound, though they may have admired their moral courage. You guys are awesome?

What about the music? Most nights after working on this book I played punk records on the stereo in my bedroom. After transcribing an interview I would often play everything I had by that record label. Many people I interviewed gave me copies of records and CDs they released. I listened to them carefully and discovered some little-known bands that I like. It was also a revelation to play four Dead Kennedys albums in a row. I listened again to records that I had bought at shows and at Who's Emma through the 1990s. This book is about record labels, but record labels are about music. At times this thought has worried me What about the music? After all, every single person I interviewed said that the reason they do this is they love the music. If that is what matters, who cares about all the rest?

Nonetheless there is a problem. Because I began to notice that the people who talked most about the Artist were often the most commercial of record labels. How to put that in question. So that bands can no longer say things like: we are on a major label now but it makes no difference to us as artists. We have complete freedom as artists.

In the 1990s there were about eight thousand record stores in the United States. There were more than four thousand musical instrument stores.[3] Kids don't buy electric guitars and drum kits just to play by themselves. They want to start a band. The fundamental reality is that there are a huge number of bands practicing and writing songs. Only some are punk and only some are serious about it. But that is still a very large number. And the main point that got repeated in every interview I did with record labels is that the social relation between the label and band is of the utmost importance. Almost nobody gets signed by sending a demo to a record label. (There are some notable exceptions especially at a small number of commercial labels that like to work with start-up bands.) But fundamentally it is a social relation. You get out there and play shows and you get to know other bands and through that kind of social network you get on a punk record label. And then you tour some more. Maybe you start to get good and then your second record sells 10,000 copies.[4]

Assuming you've been able to keep up all this and the band stays together you are now (excuse the expression) an average punk band. You're a good band but there are lots of good bands out there. If things go well and somehow you're responding to something that kids share (anger, frustration, loss, momentary bliss) and in a musical idiom that is fresh (you can't just repeat Discharge, Anti-Flag, or Fugazi) and you keep touring and people don't quit the band (because they hate you or just want to go back to college) then maybe you're a well-known punk band and your record sells 20,000 copies (punk-rock platinum). It may take a few bands to get to that stage. If you want to go further, you mostly have to move into the world of the big indie labels and a big record distributor. To avoid the distribution companies owned by the major labels will be increasingly difficult. To sign with a major label and survive as a band is a miracle.

Consider a band that is starting to move through this cycle. Right now they're on Jade Tree and surprised at where their interviews are being published. Four years ago they played a show where hardly anyone came. Now you can't get in the door. Watching all this happen from the fake interview in *Maximumrocknroll* to the professional promotion today, its hard to separate out "just the music" from these layers of social action.[5] Music is a complex form of communication and it seems difficult to completely separate it from social relations. Being in a band and making music together is an intense social relation.[6] Being friends with a small record label that you know might take your first 7" record. So it is worthwhile practicing. Being good friends with another band. That's hope. In a city that has a weekly punk show on community radio and a club with an indie-rock night on Sundays to showcase bands. That's encouragement. Is it ever possible to completely separate the music from these social relationships and organizations? Isn't music itself a social offering? Especially punk, which is often an acquired taste and intentionally excludes some listeners (you call that music) and includes others (at my first punk show I knew I was finally home).

It is sometimes said that art is about freedom. But that is much too simple. To claim to be an artist is not to leave behind the social world. Doing art is simply another more complex way of engaging with tradition and innovation, the self and others. It is not possible to appeal to a special status as a way of brushing aside ethical choices and responsibility. Artist doesn't do it. No musician is ever free on a major record label. But that does not mean that the alternatives are easy. This book has tried to describe some of those choices.

Notes

1. Michael T. Fournier, *Double Nickels on the Dime* (New York: Continuum, 2007) gives a close reading of the 1983 album by the Minutemen. The band came from working-class backgrounds and some of the songs are about the frustrations of factory jobs, about politics (El Salvador, Vietnam, the Berlin Wall), literature (James Joyce) and philosophy (Wittgenstein). But the song "Storm in My House" with guest lyrics by Henry Rollins (who came from an upper-middle class background) uses the temporary experience of working on house construction as a metaphor for personal emotions. A storm hits the exposed timbers of the house.

2. Among the labels that issued riot grrrl bands, K Records began as a tape label in Olympia, Washington, in 1982. Ian MacKaye of Dischord and Calvin Johnson of K Records had known each other since 1980. (Fugazi supported the riot grrrl movement.) Kill Rock Stars was started by Slim Moon in 1991, also in Olympia. In the mid-1990s the label was distributed by Mordam. Simple Machines in the Washing-

ton, DC area was independent but willing to work with MTV, New Music Seminar, and *College Music Journal*. See Mark Anderson and Mark Jenkins, *Dance of Days: Two Decades of Punk in the Nation's Capital* (New York: Soft Skull Press, 2001), 353–56.

3. Geoffrey P. Hull, *The Recording Industry* 2d ed. (New York and London: Routledge, 2004), 210. Some consumer music magazines have regular articles aimed at readers in bands, with advice about being in a band, equipment and success in the music industry.

4. The best book on being in a DIY punk band in the 1990s is Jon Resh, *Amped: Notes From a Go-Nowhere Punk Band* (Chicago: Viper Press, 2001).

5. There are precedents for a record-label owner interviewing a band on their label. Ian MacKaye interviewed Beefeater in *Maximumrocknroll* no. 25, May–June 1985. Available online at www.operationphoenix.com (24 April 2007). The problem here is that the band interviewed themselves.

6. Joe Carducci, *Rock and the Pop Narcotic* (Chicago: Redoubt Press, 1990). Part of this is reprinted in Clinton Heylin ed., *The Penguin Book of Rock and Roll Writing* (London: Viking, 1992), 124–50. Carducci's argument about the collective creation of rock and punk music by the band is somewhat spoiled by homophobic language throughout the book.

APPENDIX A

Interview with Lengua Armada

Martín Sorrondeguy, singer in the well-known Chicago band Los Crudos was interviewed on 26 August 2005 in Toronto where he was visiting for a show with his new band Limp Wrist. In the 1980s and 1990s Los Crudos was popular with both crust and straightedge parts of the U.S. punk scene and the band also toured internationally. The lyrics are in Spanish except for one song addressing racism in the US hardcore scene and typically deal with political issues, especially in Latin America. Limp Wrist is a queer hardcore band that confronts the scene with this issue. Martín entered the punk scene against opposition from some of his family (especially his father) but with some cultural capital even at a young age. He took photographs at shows (he later studied photography) and had the initiative to put out records. He soon gained social capital (people who helped with the records) but he also pushed the punk scene to live up to its political ideals. Lengua Armada was started as the label for Los Crudos and benefitted from the band's popularity. The record label for Martín is inseparable from his political ideals and his social networks (not exclusively punk). It is an important activity (he puts a lot of effort into it) but he distances himself from record labels that operate as business enterprises. Situated in the hardcore punk field, it is a little difficult for Martín to have to comment on individual labels. In the interview he generally expresses his values by supporting the heterodoxy of the younger generation (the kid putting out his first record) against older more established punk labels. The interview draws on a relationship that goes back ten years, occasionally meeting within the punk scene. There is a shared language: the phrase "adult crash" is from a well-known song by Minor Threat. But the interview is a very familiar convention in punk culture. Martín has been interviewed many times, especially as a member of the band Los Crudos.

Some Punk Kid in Chicago

Let's talk about the beginnings of the label. I saw from the interview that you did with Stephe Perry in Maximum *that you put out some records before Lengua Armada. How did you start?*

It started with me just being some punk kid in Chicago and wanting to do a record just focusing on Chicago bands, locally that I was going to see. It was a way for me to get to know people. I would go up to bands and say hey, I'm going to put out a record. To kind of get myself integrated a little more with what was happening in the city. So I released a compilation seven-inch with about six or seven bands, That was called *There's a Fungus Amongus*. I did a fanzine for a little while called *What the Fuck*. That's what started all that. The second release that I did was a compilation LP that was a benefit for the American Indian Treaty Right Committee. They were mainly a Midwest organization and it was a record called *Built on Blood*. That raised money for this organization. It was to get bands from all over the world to come together and focus some attention on the 500-year anniversary of the, quote, discovery of Columbus. To raise awareness among punks and young kids that this is not cool anymore. That was a really good record. I worked on that with a friend of mine, put that out. And then Lengua Armada started when Los Crudos started. [. . .]

Let's go back to the first seven-inch. Was that you were still fairly new? It was a way of participating in the scene?

I started going to shows. It was probably around eighty-five. I felt so outside of everything and was trying to get into it. At the time I still thought that punk was this really political thing. I wanted the action. I felt it wasn't happening. It wasn't coming to me and so I thought, I gotta do it then. In order to make anything happen in this world, you have to fucking do it. You have to steer the wheel.

You were fairly new to the scene and things were not moving and it was a way of participating.

Right. There was nothing coming out of Chicago. There were all these bands and we're really into them, well let's do this record. Me and a group of friends were doing this fanzine. So we put out this record. I knew nothing about how to do it. It was literally a learning process. How much does this cost? And I have to come up with this money. And then I want to make covers. I started my first homemade, handmade. . . . Somebody helped out. They worked at a print place and said I can do this print-over this color that you splashed over this paper. So everything was coming together like that.

The bands were people that you approached cold or did you know them a little bit?

By then I knew them already. They'd seen me at all those shows. I was always talking pictures. So I became this kind of familiar face at the shows. So that comp was Screaching Weasel, Gear . . . there were a bunch of bands. They already knew who I was.

Photography was a way of participating as well.

Yes, by taking the camera to the shows I was always upfront by the stage or to the side of the stage. It became this thing, hey there's Martín. The scene at the time had become very suburban because the city seemed all about money at that point and bigger shows. We were a group of kids from the city going to the suburbs. And they were there's who lives in the city. And this is his sister. And I was always there taking pictures and dancing along. That's kind of how it happened.

You would have been pretty young?

I was probably 17 when I started going to shows.

How much would you have needed to put the record out? Two thousand?

Not even that much. It was a seven-inch so it was probably $800 or thereabout.

So it was doable?

It was doable. I can't even remember how I got that money. Now that I think about it, I don't know how the hell I got that money. I wasn't bus-boying then because I had a mohawk. You know I was working at, believe it or not, a gun club. Because no one else would hire me. It was a gun club in the middle of winter that allowed me to wear my hat. I was a pull boy. There were these fuckers there with their shotguns or rifles and they would say "pull" so they could shoot their little clay dogs. [laughs] And that's how I got money and that's how the record came about.

So it was your job, you saved your money. Can you remember how many copies you would have put out?

The first seven-inch. If I'm not mistaken there were a thousand made. Five hundred to a thousand. I think it was a thousand.

You had no problem selling them?

I got rid of them. I got rid of a certain amount and I was sitting on four or five hundred or something and then over time they went. I don't know how that all happened but yeah, I got rid of them.

It was a good experience. It encouraged you.

To want to do it more. It did. I got really discouraged when I did the *Built on Blood* record. Because I had really really bad experiences with the pressing plant. And when you're just some kid who's putting out a record they really will treat you like shit. They don't care. Because you're not a big account for them. I got a pressing of a thousand LPs and eight, nine hundred were warped. I was fighting with them, it was so stressful, at that age I thought I was going to have a heart attack I was so stressed about it. No, I need these records replaced. Just going on and on with them about it.

You were just a kid.

They could have just gone, fuck you. And they were almost like that. We would get in a shouting match. I'm like, I can't believe I have to do this.

Did you have to pay upfront?

Well you do. Usually you have to pay half upfront. But at that time I think I paid a good portion of that upfront. I kinda learned as I went along what to do, what not to do. And with the booklets some print shop wanted to charge me a thousand dollars for these booklets and luckily I met some guy who worked at Kinkos who hated his job and said I will do your booklets for free. Within a week I had a thousand booklets. He saved me. I couldn't even think about coming up with another grand. [laughs]

That one sold as well?

Everything sold. Everything eventually. It did have its slow points but for the most part that one did well. It had a lot of bands like Filth and Misery and across the board. It was an expensive record. It was an LP and a seven-inch. I wanted to do this benefit and it was an awareness thing, and I still managed to raise over a thousand dollars for the American Indian Treaty Rights Committee which was a significant amount of money for them, because it was a non-profit.

And the first seven-inch was like Dischord? Documenting your scene, documenting Chicago. Have you continued with that?

I do that, I still do it but in a different way. I tend to release bands, not exclusively, but I like to release bands from places I lived if possible. So I'll still release some Chicago bands for friends. I'm doing a single soon by some LA bands that I'm friends with, or played with, or hung out with. Stuff like that. I was doing international stuff. I did a band from Mexico, from Israel. Doing the Histeria compilations I have bands from all over the world.

So Lengua Armada started with Los Crudos?

It did. We started the band and we really thought in all honesty that people weren't going to give a shit, especially in the States. A band that sings in Spanish, who cares? We thought it was just going to be a neighbourhood thing. When it came time that we were ready to release our first record, we said well, let's put it out ourselves. I told them I had already done a record. We did it and I came up with the name of the label because I'd seen an old FSLN record called Guitarra Armada but I thought is it the guitars that are armed or is it what comes out of the vocalist that is armed. *Lengua armada.* That's where I came up with that. We released the first Crudos single under the name Lengua Armada.

What is the relationship between the band and the label? Is the label more your project?

At first it was kind of our project. Let's do this label. Within a short period of time the guys realized they just weren't interested. We would do the handmade record covers and when you start doing that and it's two thousand copies, it's work. Doing the mail and everything. I kind of adopted it and made it more, I kept going with it whereas other people fell off, they weren't as interested. But even through to about '96 when the LP came out they were still all helping. It wasn't like this was mine, they were helping too. But I did all the mail, all the mail order, taking care of the official stuff.

Their helping out was a kind of work bee, doing the crafts, the silk-screening, the hand-made. . . .

They helped out with that but there was so much of a crossing with the band and the label. They might come over to make shirts or records and the shirts were for the band. I never made a Lengua Armada t-shirt. It was just Los Crudos, that's what we did. So they were involved. Other random kids would come over and help us out. I'll help you do this. Or I'll help you do mail. People helping me, because they knew I was swamped.

Los Crudos became very popular. Is it true to say that was the foundation of Lengua Armada, the popularity of Los Crudos?

It helped Lengua Armada. It also was good for us because we basically were in complete control of what was happening with our music and we were very happy about that. We had total say about what was going on with our records. If we didn't agree with the way somebody wanted to distribute our records we just wouldn't send any to them. Because the band was touring and playing so much. It made it possible for us to really sell directly to kids. Our LPs were five dollars, which is really cheap. Seven-inches were on average three dollars, t-shirts were five dollars. Everything was cheap. We made it as accessible as we could.

How many releases are you up to now? Thirty five, close to forty?

Close to forty. It's thirty-nine or something.

You said the label is based in places that you're living or people that you know. Is Lengua Armada also about a type of music? A genre of music?

It's definitely, the music is definitely connected to hardcore punk. I've done stuff that is a little heavier but it's definitely in the punk vein. And if it wasn't musically punk or as classically punk, politically it was punk, attitude-wise it was punk. I wouldn't put out a band that played fast hardcore if they sung about stupid things. Lengua Armada definitely had an agenda, what we're willing to support and not support. If you were misogynist or whatever, racist, homophobic, you know, fuck that. We wouldn't release your record. We're not interested in your band.

So fast hardcore usually with some kind of a political message.

Oh definitely. Hardcore punk and definitely have some good message. It didn't have to be overtly political. It could have been more of a social, you know political . . . but some of it was heavy-duty political.

Is that how you would think about the label, not so much a straight-edge or a Chicago label.

No. We were a punk label. And our vision was more global than local. We did do a lot of Chicago bands but we did bands from everywhere. I released a band from Spain, Israel, from Mexico. I started really broadening that by having bands from everywhere.

Do you think people understand what to expect from a Lengua Armada record?

I think so. People know. It does have an identity. I think people go, this is Martín's shit. [laughs] He's into this. I think over the years I've released a few things that were maybe not overtly political but there was definitely some message in there or something that I was just into. Or really sarcastic, or their delivery was really fucking with stuff. But I think people know. I guess people have paid attention to it over the years and I'm lucky for that. Because they could have ignored it if they wanted.

That Label Is More about Moving Units

Epitaph. You were saying that you're not quite sure what they are doing. It seems to be mostly about selling records.

At this point that label is more about moving units. I'm sure that somebody at that label likes the bands but it seems like the popular bands that they know sell. I think that the difference between what I do is that there could be a band and I don't give a shit if it's going to sell. I'm into it and I want to release it because I'm that into it, because it's something that I feel is important.

For you, is Epitaph part of the scene?

No. They're not. I don't think so. They're not a part of my scene. I don't know those people individually, personally. But what they do as their work I don't associate with it.

What about Dischord? They're about documenting a scene in Washington and you started out documenting a scene in Chicago.

Dischord. I like Dischord. Musically I was more interested in early Dischord. Ideally I would like Dischord and respect Dischord. Am I interested in all of it? No I'm not. But I can put that aside and go looking at what they have done and be to a certain degree intrigued, interested and influenced by the way that they have done things. But there are a lot of labels I can think of that have done things like that. But Dischord is a good example.

Have you ever talked with them?

Hmm. I met Ian when Fugazi came on the first tour to Chicago. But it's not like I have ever hung out for a long period of time with them or anything like that. Took photos of them and stuff.

They have an office and at least one fulltime person.

It's organized. I also think, they advertise. They advertise a lot in different magazines. Not more than Epitaph. They do a good job in remaining DIY, doing things themselves and getting it out there.

How about Felix Havoc?

You know, I like what he does musically. He really gets his stuff out all over the place. It just gets everywhere. I like what he does with his label. I can respect what he does and I like the bands that he releases.

Can you come up with a label that you think is pretty similar to what you are trying to do?

[pause] A label that comes to mind is Reacciona from Mexico. These are old friends of ours, we lived together for a while. They are from Monterey. They've been doing some really cool stuff. Not just releasing records. They're renting busses and getting bands together to tour Mexico. It's not just about, we do a record label. They organize tours, they organize everything just because they feel they need it. Just to bring stuff to people there. Because it's sort of limited what they get. So I love Reacciona. There's other . . . I'm really into young, new, energetic labels that come up. I like supporting a kid who releases his first record and say I'll trade you. Doing that swapping. I like La Vida Es Un Mus. He's from Spain, moved to London, he's back in Spain now. He does things in a cool way. I like what he releases. He's a great person. That's how I would gauge: do I like a label, do I like the people who do it.

There is a bunch. There is a lot of newer . . . the old established labels you know it's kind of weird. It's a little difficult for me because a lot of the labels that started around when I started, most of them kind of surrendered. They started doing exclusive distribution, they don't want to be bothered dealing directly with the kids. I was always annoyed by that and I was always put off by that because it's almost a slap in the face to everybody that helped build what you have. So I kinda was critical of that and I never wanted to become that and I never did. So when everybody was doing exclusive distribution that literally eliminated the possibility of everyday punk kids going to shows and getting your music, I was really fucking annoyed by that. So I didn't care where somebody was writing me from saying all I can sell is five copies. Hey, I'll send you five copies. I'll send you three copies, I don't care. I still to this day like to do that if possible.

Both of the examples that you name are not from the United States.

I'm sure that there are some record labels in the States that I like, you know.

I thought you might have said Ebullition. They are bigger though.

Kent has been extremely important for what has been happening DIY-wise in the United States for a long time. I think maybe things have shifted a little bit. He's still doing what he has been doing. The thing is that they are so huge in being a distributor that I don't think Kent has much time to do much more than that. I respect what he does. I think things have shifted a little bit though where he's not doing the show stuff anymore. His operation is huge.

When you started was there a label that you modeled yours on or looked up to?

I can't right now remember if there was a certain label that I looked up to. Because everything at that time seemed big to me. Everything was official. People ran their labels officially, had an official logo. Until this day there isn't a Lengua Armada logo. I don't care. There are fuck ups all over my releases and I almost applaud them when I find them. Where I will simply leave out a contact address. Or I won't even put the label name on the record. I love that kind of anonymous, it just is what it is. I did the Tragatelo twelve-inch and it does not say Lengua Armada anywhere on it. People are, I didn't know that was your record. [laughs] Or I have another record from Japan and it says Lengua Armada but it's not in English so no American kids can look at it and say oh did this. It's what it is, you know. On those records too there are mistakes, things left out.

I've only done one ad since the label started and that was for the first Crudos single and I've never done an ad since then. Which is kind of funny but then it's word of mouth, people being dedicated enough supporting it.

Maybe that's because you're not trying to make a living from it.

Absolutely. I have a very different attitude. If I were to think about conversations I had with people about their labels, I think a lot of label people have this tendency to believe that they released the band's record and therefore they kind of own the band. And I don't believe that at all. The band has the right to do what they want with their music. The artist has that say. Yes, I supported you but I don't think you have to be loyal to me. In that sense my attitude is very different. I don't make a living from the label. I don't have to promote, promote, promote. It's not a business. My interests are maybe not the same as somebody else doing a record label.

We Were Friends

Let's talk about the relationship between the label and the bands. Let's start with the split record between Los Crudos and MK-Ultra.[1] How did that come about in terms of the relation between you putting that out and the guys in the band.

We were friends. We played together all the time. It was a time when Los Crudos was popular enough that we could support these local bands. So we always had these young bands playing with us. MK-Ultra and Charles Bronson those were all bands, there were so many more, we would just put them on these shows. It was really a great time for us and them. It brought in all their friends, yet they'd be playing to two, three hundred people. If they did a show on their own it would be twenty people, twenty-five people. So it was supporting, inviting them on tour . . .

When did it come out?

This actually came out not too long ago. It's old material. This was recorded right before Crudos broke up, among the last songs we recorded. We had been talking about doing the release forever. Finally it came out.

So the relationship was they were friends of Los Crudos, they played with Los Crudos.

And we liked what the band was about. We liked what MK-Ultra was about. They definitely took a stance on something and we're like, let's do this record together.

How many bands on the label would you say fit into that category? People that had played with Los Crudos or were friends with Los Crudos? Was it most?

Most. Absolutely. Definitely most. Most of them at one point or another we had played together, pen-palled, know what I mean? There definitely had to be some sort of connection. It was never that we got this random tape and I'm going to release this record. I would do homework: who are these guys? What are they about? What's going on with this band?

So the majority of people on Lengua Armada, there was a social network or a friendship network in place through Los Crudos?

Yes, definitely.

What about the Histeria *comps that you are doing now? Is that the same?*

Yes, they are all. . . . Well, with these bands, let me see the first one that I did, we knew everybody in these bands, or had played with them, or had booked their show or something [looks at the LP]. This is post-Crudos but some of these bands we definitely played with like Seein Red, E-150 I released their single, Seein Red we had played with, Life's Halt are LA kids that we had met already: everybody here. Esperanza had members, one of the members had booked a Crudos show in LA and we were friends with them.

He helped me with my video documentary, driving me around LA. Sin Orden are new young Latino punk kids from the neighborhood. Putting them on this was like, against this attitude that older punks have that here's these new kids: I have nothing to do with them. No, these are new kids in my fucking neighborhood. I need to nurture that. There was a connection. Death Threat we played with them all the time.

Histeria no. 2 was a little different. Fuerza X I had met them already. They were from Guatemala and I had seen them play and all that. I Quit! I don't personally know these guys. They are from Sweden, they are really cool. All their songs are anti-war songs. People told me they're good. I found out. Disidencía are from Uruguay and the guitarist from this band ended up moving to California and we started a band together. You know, everybody on here pretty much I saw or helped out, they stayed at my house. Punch in the Face is ex-Crudos drummer's band.

Do kids send you demo tapes? What do you do with them?

Yes. I say thank-you for sending me your demo. I say thanks or I liked it. You get stuff all the time. And occasionally there will be something that is really good and you say what is this? One good example is we will be releasing a seven-inch by a band called Outrage. I got this demo and I was like, this band reminds me of Sin Orden. Are they Spanish? Where are they from? They're from Watsonville, California. Watsonville California is a migrant community. It's all farmers, they're all pickers. So I was almost immediately get in touch with these kids. Let's talk to them. Sure enough their parents all work the fields. They were these young Latino kids and it was in the middle of nowhere. I'm so blown away by this. So I'm releasing a seven-inch of theirs. Love them. I think they're great. Stuff like that will come my way and I'm like, I've got to put this out.

Relationship between the label and the bands. Written contract?

No. Not at all. Never.

Do people talk to you about arrangements, about money?

Money, how I do it? Yeah, I basically tell the band, you have this recording, I'll give you 20 percent of the pressing. So if I do a thousand records they get 200 that they can sell to make back their costs. That's kind of the agreement.

They pay for the master tape?

They usually have a recording. Or they'll record for it. If they need more copies they get them at cost. Sometimes with some bands, honestly, I end up giving more copies away. Here, I have another hundred, just take them. I kind of don't care. By that point I've probably made my money back and I'm happy.

You've never paid a band in cash?

No, I don't think so. I'm trying to think if I've ever done a combination of copies and money. For the most part the band prefers, they make out better if they get the records. If it's a seven-inch they can sell it for three bucks and they make out better.

You're not the kind of label that gives tour support?

No. Tour support for me is to make sure they have enough records to go. If they need help booking shows I will help them out. Again, the scene's weird sometimes. With Sin Orden for example they were just killing people in Chicago, people were freaking out on how good they were and going crazy for them. I tried to book their shows on the East Coast and no one would book them. I was really upset about it. These are people who I had known for a while. I was sitting there with the kids in my house. We had no luck. Nobody is responding. I said let me make calls and I started calling and people were so disinterested. What are they like? And I'm like, they're Latino hardcore. I don't know what they interpreted by that but no one would book them. And I just looked at these kids and I said, you know what, fuck all these people. I said fuck everyone. Don't go on tour. Wait about another year and they're going to call you. Fuck them. That was kind of my attitude with Crudos. You know, fuck everybody. If they don't like it too bad. The reverse happened. People were like, we want you to play. I think that is what is happening now. They've got back together playing shows and it's starting to happen.

So the way you can help a band touring is through your contacts, helping to set up a tour?

Yeah, stuff like that. I can't afford to help a band buy a van. I don't go out and make tour posters. For a show I will do it and I can organize a band's show in my town or my city and do a really good job on it. But I'm not, you know. If they want to make t-shirts we can make t-shirts. But I don't do this major tour support thing, no.

The label doesn't make band t-shirts.

I've helped. When Sin Orden were just starting out and they were literally, how do we start? And I said come over and we made a stencil out of contact paper and made a screen. Like really raw. One of them knew how to draw Sin

Orden. And we literally sprayed or screened these little shirts with Sin Orden on them. They sold them to their friends, which gave them the money to record their first demo. I'm not going to do everything for a band. I like that people learn how to do these things. That is a better example to set. Survival of a band on its own without everybody fucking doing things for you. If you want everybody to do everything for you then why even be in a punk band? Go ahead and try to be a major-label band. Whatever.

The commitment is for one record and to help people out a bit? One seven-inch or one album?

I've done multiple releases. For Look Back and Laugh, I did two of them. And they were really happy and I was really excited to work with them and let's just do it. We've gotten rid of everything. It hasn't been a problem. I love the band, they're great people. I'm into what they're doing. They could easily be on any label they want. Seriously they could just pick any label they want. But the fact is, we've worked well together. I'm not hard to work with. I do whatever bands want. If you want to do this, yeah we can really do it. We did a five-screen job on their first record and I sat there silk-screening with them. I flew to the Bay area to silk-screen their record covers. I'm dedicated to what I do.

How would you have felt if they had moved to another record label?

You know they've released some songs on other labels. A split record with Dropdead. I'm trying to remember if they did something else. Damn it, I don't own them. The band can do what they want.

Would you expect them to give you a call or something?

What happens is I say, you're doing another recording, are you going to have somebody else release it? I'd be into doing it if you still want me to. I love your band or whatever. And if they're going to do something with another label, okay it's cool. I can't personalize that. A band is free to do what they want.

Have you ever toured with a band on the label?

Just me going along with the band? I can't do that any more. I can't really survive. I have to work and I don't have that much free time. I did go on a little tour for several days with E-150 when they came from Spain, you know, stuff like that. I went up to Michigan with them and then when they went into Canada I came back. They had people helping them out and one or two of them spoke English okay.

I Personally Love Vinyl

Let's talk about formats. Cassettes?

We start with a demo tape sometimes.

You have put out tapes?

They were not official Lengua Armada releases. Crudos did a demo tape. It wasn't like it was Lengua Armada no. 1 or anything. It was a demo tape. Did a Limp Wrist demo tape. Couple of things like that.

How do you feel about cassettes?

I love cassettes. What I think about a cassette. It's cheap, the quality is not supreme. But the fact is that most punk in Third World nations was cassette-based. It was accessible, it was affordable, it was totally economical. It was a very good way of getting music here and there and swapping. You fit a lot of it on a tape. It's cheap. And on the other hand because most Latin American or Third World punk came out on cassettes a lot of it is lost. A lot of the original recordings have degraded, just lost. So if somebody were to try to do a retrospective of Argentinean punk it would be really hard to dig up a lot of that. But I like the cassette.

How many would you do if you put out a cassette? Two hundred?

Yeah, maybe two or three hundred, depending on how it was doing. I think Tragatelo which is another band from LA, I didn't release the cassette, friends did. But five hundred were sold of the cassette in Japan alone. It's kinda weird. I was shocked to hear that. Five hundred in Japan alone. I just thought that was wild. So it depends. A couple of hundred.

CDs.

You know, I've only done one CD, two CDs. The Los Crudos discography CD because we had to. It had to be done. I've never been a big CD person. I love the CD-R now. I do. Because I love burning music without having to spend a shit load of money. So that's a brilliant thing. I personally am not interested in the CD market. I think it is a huge sham. It's so cheap to produce yet they just kill people with what they charge for it. So my thing is that I wanted to do the CD for Crudos to make everything available. I can't keep pressing the vinyl. There's just too much. It's too expensive, too much work. So we did the CD discography of that. We did the Limp Wrist discography. That was a four-label collaboration. And those are the only two CDs that I believe I was involved with.

Dischord seems to be using the CD in that way, to bring together a discography. That seems useful.

It is. And what they were doing it with, that stuff is so unobtainable now. Those singles, if you want to sit around on E-Bay and pay a couple of hundred bucks you can get those records. That is so counter-punk. So them doing those CDs is smart.

So for you it is about vinyl.

I love vinyl. Personally I love vinyl. These days kids come up to me and say I'm sorry but I downloaded your stuff. I don't care: that's cool. I really don't care. I'm for downloading. Hey man if you can get any of my music for free, just get it. That means I didn't have to go to all this work to mail it to you, you send me money. No just get it from the computer and you have it. I'm fine with that. I don't need royalties. If you're making money from it, I'll be, hey man that sucks. But if the kid can get it for free. . . . I'm all about trading, swapping and all that.

There's still places that press vinyl? It's not a problem?

No it's not a problem.

In Spain there is nowhere left. They have to send to Germany and that increases the cost because you have to pay taxes and shipping.

I think the Czech Republic is still doing cheap vinyl. It's very affordable. In the States it's not a problem. As a matter of fact, the punk scene, our scene [. . .] The number of people actually buying music, paying for it, has declined. Labels are decreasing their pressing numbers. Which brings up different issues such as limited accessibility. But the label has to consider that I do not want to sit on 500 copies of a record for the rest of my life.

What is your normal edition for a Lengua Armada record?

I'd say that for a seven-inch for a newer band it would be a thousand copies. I have some that I'm going to do soon and it's dropping down to five, six hundred copies. [. . .] I'm doing a band from Israel and their chances of touring here are really slim so I might just do five hundred. I'm doing a single by an old Uruguayan band from '85 that got censored a while back and I'm doing five hundred. It's punk not hardcore but it's really cool. And I'm doing a couple of other projects like that.

And twelve-inch?

Yeah, I'm still doing twelve-inch records. Numbers? For Look Back and Laugh because they are very popular I did 1,500 copies and I might do 500 more.

Can I ask you what did Los Crudos sell? Your best selling record? Did you get up to ten thousand?

Past. That was because we had other labels release also. There would be a European pressing of the record, we would do our pressings, somebody in Japan would do a pressing, somebody in Poland would do it on cassette, that kind of thing. So when you take all those numbers into consideration the Los Crudos LP probably sold sixteen, seventeen thousand.

How does that relationship with those other labels work? Do you just allow them freely to put it out?

They ask. They call us or send a letter and say I really want to release your band. They tend to introduce themselves. Okay sure. You see if they are really serious about it and then you let them do it. For a cassette release in Malaysia or something if they just send us each one or two copies each of the cassette we're happy. We don't need a cut, you know. It's never been like that.

There is no royalty payment or twenty percent.

It's only happened with like the CD release in Spain, the Crudos discography. I learned the hard way that you have to, in certain circumstances you have to discuss that. Because the Crudos '90 to '95 album, the discography of the singles and all that, it got released in Europe and there were something like five, six thousand copies made there and the guy who organized it all wanted to send us ten copies. And I was like you're crazy. And he ended up saying, okay I'll send you a hundred and we'll work out a trade. And I was no, you made six thousand copies of an LP that fucking sold out. You know, that's going to sell out. That relationship was severed because we were so offended that he would have done that. We felt really cheated on that.

It would seem justified for you to ask for what is in effect a royalty.

It didn't have to be in cash. It could have been in records. I'd be fine with that. But the fact is this particular person didn't feel that he needed to do that. You're crazy. We were under the assumption that this person did things the way we did. It's just a given that you would give the band copies. Even if it was ten percent of the entire pressing, which would have been 600 copies of an album. No, he only gave us a hundred. We're still talking about that he should give us copies of something in trade. This a vinyl record that came out a while back.

What happened with the European CD full discography?

They were really good with us. They said what do you want, do you want copies or the money. It was easier at that point for us to get money. We just got some money for it. [. . .]

The scene is based on trust. But sometimes you have to put down some boundaries and say, well no, that is kind of ripping us off. The label can always use copies or the cash to put out something else that is going to lose money.

You have to communicate that. You have to. And you can't just assume. It has to be brought up.

Are you able to keep stuff in print? Does it go out of print real fast?

It goes out of print. I have this thing, I stay away from my records being in quarter bins if possible. Where things are over-pressed. There may be some more interest down the line where, you know, I could probably press another five hundred and sell it. But is that ten years later? Come on! I'm not going to do that. It's like, are you excited? Pick it up when it's there. And that's kind of the way punk is. It's been like that, you get it.

What's your feeling about price? For you a seven-inch should be?

Three dollars. I still sell my seven-inches for three dollars. [A retail price of US$3] Most of the new kids who do records sell them for four dollars. I get kinda pissed. I do because I used to be able to get three seven-inches for ten dollars. And now to get three seven-inches it's twelve dollars. I'm not a wealthy person. I don't have a lot of money. As records get more expensive I become more selective about what I buy. Whereas I used to buy everything before, I don't do that anymore. [. . .] I'm not buying as much. I can't afford it. I had this one band, this person say, "Do you do international trading." And there was this person there who said, "Do you know who the fuck you're talking to?" He was like, how dare you. He was really offended. "This guy has been doing international trading forever."

And a twelve-inch? How much do you sell them for?

That one, it used to be six. At this point they are probably seven or eight. But I'll sometimes still go to a show and twelve-inches are six bucks. People are like huh? Seven or eight, it just depends. But it's not more than eight, never. Even if it's a trade for some international record, you know.

Would that be in part the criteria you would use in judging another label?

There's labels I like that the records are more expensive. Nine dollars or twelve dollars. It's just for me. I feel better. I can cover all my costs and still keep things relatively cheap. I've been told that my prices are so old school.

How about distribution? It sounds like that in the beginning a lot of it was bringing your crates to Los Crudos shows.

A lot of it was. We probably got rid of a majority of our own records, just going to shows and selling them.

And the label as well?

Definitely. That's how we got rid of most of our stuff.

Do you use a distributor?

Yeah. I do Ebullition. He's the main person but I also deal with a lot of overseas people in smaller quantity.

How many typically would Ebullition take? Would they take a hundred seven-inches?

It depends. Like the new Look Back and Laugh record, they took seven hundred. That's a twelve inch record and of 1,500 they took seven hundred.

They took half the pressing.

Totally. He knew it was going to sell. [. . .] If there was a smaller, unknown band he would take two hundred.

Beyond that most of your stuff is small-scale trades, other small labels around the world, barter.

Sometimes it's five.

For trades do you question what they are going to send you?

Tell me what it is. My criteria is, is it punk, is it hardcore. I don't want metal, I don't want grind, I don't want crossover, new metal. I'm not into any of that. If it's hardcore punk I'm willing to check it out. Sometimes my curiosity is peaked about what that band is about or like. And then, you know, sometimes I can't sell them. I end up setting up a bin somewhere at a show with things for cheap to get rid of them. I've had LPs for two or three dollars just to get rid of them. People are unfamiliar, people don't take chances all the time. I have to sometimes tell kids, this is an amazing record. Seriously, it's like this, this, this.

People know your tastes and think if he likes it I'll probably like it.

That can sometimes happen. I can say if you're really into this kind of stuff, you should really check this out, you'll be into this.

Do you ever say no to trades?

Yeah. I do say no. Especially right now because of my move and everything, I'm not doing the distro so much. I've been a little more hesitant to do trades because I don't have room for it, I haven't been going to shows much right now and distroing. It would be too much for me to take on.

It's mostly trades, so you don't have problems getting paid. I assume Kent [Ebullition Distribution] is good at paying.

He's good at that, that's not an issue.

What about promotion. You mostly leave that to the band. Because you don't take out ads.

I haven't done that. I keep on saying I'm going to. For the last three or four years I've been saying, I should send an ad in. But I haven't done that.

You don't send promotional copies.

Just for *Maximumrocknroll*, Ebullition's *Heartattack* zine.

So you do send out promotional copies to these two zines. Punk Planet? That's outside of your. . . .

Kinda. Sorta. I don't think they're interested in the kind of stuff that I release too much. I don't recall ever sending them anything.

That's pretty focused in terms of promotion.

Slug and Lettuce. Chris will get stuff from me. I'm trying to think who else. I'll give stuff away if I find a kid who is doing a zine or something. I give stuff away all the time.

Informally. But you don't have a computerized list.

No I don't [laughs].

Is there a radio show in Chicago, or now in San Francisco?

Well, Maximumrocknroll radio. So they get my stuff. I normally would send MRR a stack, so that other people can get copies, like shit workers.

It's not fulltime work, it's never been fulltime work.

Sometimes it felt like fulltime work.

Because you always had a job. How many hours a week? Lets say when the label was very busy.

It is hard to answer. When things were really busy? Let's take when the Crudos LP came out, the thick cardboard one. We screened three colors, two or three screens on that and that was six thousand of them. So we had to do them a few hundred now, a few hundred then. Things were moving so fast and people wanted so many. The mail was coming in. It was just like, I would come home from work from teaching and just be checking my messages, opening up the mail. Oh shit these guys need a hundred, two hundred. I need to send Kent a whole bunch. I make a few calls. I really need help. People would come over and help me screen.

Packaging them, getting them to the post office

Going with a cart because I didn't have a car. Seeing if somebody could get me a ride to get hundreds of records to the post office. Packing a grocery cart with them or just packing my bags up.

You still must spend a couple of hours a week on the label today.

More than that. Many, many hours. But it was fun. I would have people come over and it was almost like we were socializing. Busting our asses but then take a break to eat, hang out or whatever. Now it has been harder for me because I live by myself and I'm getting tired of doing this. It's really a lot of time and a lot of work. I get frustrated. When a record is done though I'm like [sighs with relief] that's cool. It's kind of a reward the feeling of I've made it happen.

It's never gotten to the stage that you said you needed someone to work twenty hours a week and you're going to pay them?

No.

It's always been phoning friends and asking for help.

Or people offering to help. It was kinda cool.

Do you have a website?

No. Don't want to, don't care. [laughs] A website would be interesting for me if it were a historical archive type of thing. And I could get criticized for that.

People could say, you would sell so much shit. But, I don't know. I'm just not kinda, I'm just not that interested in it. Again I think that would push me into running things like a business and I don't want to. I don't want to be a legitimate, this serious fucking record label. I think punks are drawn to it because of that. Because it's not this, I'm not trying to sell you this record, I'm not all about. . . . It's just a different trip, you know. For some reason it's worked for me. It may not work for everybody. It doesn't work for everybody. But for me it has worked and I'm happy with that.

You've never done a catalogue?

No. I do little mail order slips that I throw in when somebody orders, a little flyer. This is what I have. I like them. It goes in a letter.

You've Been Asked This a Million Times

You've been asked this a million times. How did you get involved in punk? You grew up in Chicago.

My first exposure to punk was when I was a kid. I was really young and my cousins were into punk but in New York. I was in fifth grade then when I first heard of punk. And I thought it was cool. Anything that came in my direction as a kid that was punk or new wave, I thought it was cool and I was really into it. But my leanings based on where I was, the time, I got into the earliest of the B-boy scene, the hiphop scene and break dancing. That's kind of what I was into because it was there. There were no punks living in my neighborhood. That was nonexistent. By the time the whole b-boy thing was falling off around the end of '84 and I said I'm going punk. And people thought I was crazy. I knew this is where I needed to go and that's where I went.

You've talked about this elsewhere, it was difficult with your parents, especially with your dad.

Yeah, really difficult. My dad thought the punk thing was a gay thing. Which later on, it wasn't then, it became that later, but he couldn't deal with the whole, why is he doing this to himself. There were moments when it was literally physical, where I'd get into a fight with my dad. He would say after a while, I know you're dirty but you're not like those people on the North side. I'm like, I do go to the North side sometimes but what do you mean? I think he was really afraid of it. He wouldn't walk on the same side of the street as I. If we were going somewhere together it was you stay here, I'm going over there. He didn't want to be seen with me. We had our tough times. Over time though it took care of itself. And now, fuck, if I were to go home like this with my mohawk, he likes it now. I went home with half a head of hair and he goes [gasps] you look like Taxi Driver. He's into it, you know. And when I started getting rid of my long hair or stopped dying my hair, he was like, what are you doing? You're looking so normal. That's not you. Where he finally came around to it. It took time.

Both your parents were immigrants to the States?

Yes. I was born in Uruguay and they brought us all over. We all came together.

What does your Dad do?

My dad is a carpenter and cabinet-maker.

Does he work for himself?

Yes, for himself. He's always been his own boss.

How far did he get in school?

I think sixth grade.

He would have had an apprenticeship as a carpenter.

Yeah, something like that. He stopped his education really early. Whereas my Mum was in medical school. She wanted to become a doctor.

But she wasn't able to finish.

She decided to do the family, months, months before receiving her degree.

What does she do now? Does she work?

No, my mum hasn't worked for a while. For quite some time she worked for an organization called Mujeres Latinas en Acción. They did prenatal class work, going to high schools doing outreach to girls about protecting themselves. And this was during mid- to late seventies, eighties. And then she stopped working [. . .]

What did your parents think about the label? Did they understand what you were doing?

I think everything was a little baffling to them. What is he doing? What is he doing now? I think they kinda learned as I learned it, as I went along. I think they started to go, you got a letter today from Russia, from Japan. What is he doing? Where is this coming from? I think they were just going, huh? I remember one day my dad saying to me, I think somebody had brought it up, what do you think about all this stuff does? My dad said I can't criticize what you do. You've seen so much more of this world, I'll never have the chance to see what you've seen. So how can I criticize that. Which is really awesome, you know.

It was a matter of them learning with you, gradually understanding or would you say they encouraged it?

Oh they did. At the beginning I think they were a bit scared. What is he doing? What's going on? A little nervous, a little scared. But I always wanted to do things.

You're this kid, you're seventeen, working this job at the rifle range, you're saving up your money and then you're blowing all your money on something really weird.

Yeah, really. I wonder [laughs] I think they were really confused by a lot of it. But overall, over time my parents know a lot about fucking punk. I would even put them up against some punks. We had bands coming and staying at our house from all over the world. My parents would sit there and talk to people, talk to the punks. There's definitely, my mum gets it.

You have a degree in fine arts?

I have a Masters in fine arts. I did that at the University of Illinois in Chicago.

What was your BA?

It was a bachelor of arts from Columbia College in Chicago, mainly focused on photography, video, a little bit of everything but that was my major.

Are you the only kid in your family to go to university?

I was the first one. I was the first one to graduate from college. [. . .] I think they were really happy.

Because that's understood. Everyone can understand getting your degree but putting out punk records is a little weird.

I think that over time, because it's so many years doing it, that after a while they realized, okay he's doing his thing, it's happening.

Now you're just starting part-time teaching at a high school and you have a punk job.

Yes I'm teaching at a high school and I work for *Maximumrocknroll*.

That's an interesting place to end up.

Yeah, it really is. It's funny, I saw Martin Sprouse, who is an old-timer at *Maximum*. He came over one day and he said we were wondering how long it was going to take you before you got here. He said we've been wanting you to come here for a long time. Really. It was weird, you know. I just thought it was weird. And it's weird how I came around to that. Because I've always loved *Maximumrocknroll*, you know. It played an important part for me of. . . .

How did that come about? You knew them? You talked? Did you send a resume?

No, they sent me a questionnaire. They knew I was having some problems with my relationship at the time. They knew I was considering moving to San Francisco. [. . .] They sent me a questionnaire. They were looking for a distribution coordinator and they asked me if I would be interested and I said yes. I filled out the questions, they did a phone interview, they flew me over and interviewed me. And on my birthday I got this call, yeah you got it. [. . .]

And you have the other side too, the teaching side.

I have a lot of sides. [laughs]

And you're going to bring the punk thing into your teaching because you're going to get the kids to write a zine. You're going to talk about subcultures. You can bring this into your teaching.

Subcultures in general. It is also about these movements, what are these little movements, somewhat political, radical. What is going on? Why has this been happening in the U.S. since the fifties? Why are these movements constantly springing up? Looking at that. I do integrate the politics, the punk and all that. Where do you fit in or don't you? Just ask those questions.

I would guess that you're probably not earning as much as you could.

I'm not. I definitely don't make what other people make at all. That's been a little frustrating for me. I'm getting closer to my forties. I think within a year I'll be in school again to get my teacher's credentials to teach full time. It's definitely something I've been wanting to do and I've been thinking a lot about it.

It's the adult crash.

I guess so. Some people get it at twenty-five, some people get it at thirty, I'm getting it at forty. It's either that or I'm just going to live this crazy bohemian punk. . . . And that's just difficult. It's really hard. I've been working with kids in schools on and off for the last twelve years. What am I waiting for?

Hopefully you will still be able to bring the attitude and some of the material.

I think so. I think it can happen. It's not that I can bring the material in, but it will come up in discussion. Every teacher that I have had, depending on the class, you had discussion time and in discussion time you talk about experiences, exposure, just different things. It will come up.

Is there anything else you want to say about the label?

You know, as long as I come across people and music that is interesting, that is energetic, that is fresh, and I don't mean like they reinvented the wheel, but the energy, that energy that you get, I will continue to release records. I thought a couple of years ago that I was going to stop. And I said I was going to. But stuff kept coming at me. I gotta do this. I have to do this. I still am into what I do.

Note

1. MK-Ultra was the code name for a CIA mind-control research program that began in the 1950s. The Chicago hardcore band MK-Ultra should not to be confused with the San Francisco indie-rock band MK Ultra that existed from 1994–1999.

APPENDIX B

Record Labels Interviewed and Statistical Data

The sample of 61 record labels was constructed from knowledge of the field, from ads in major punk zines in 2006, and from the listings on Book Your Own Fucking Life. Ads in zines and record reviews were the most important source: *Maximumrocknroll, Heartattack, Profane Existence, Punk Planet, Razorcake* and *Short, Fast and Loud*. The sample includes four labels in Spain and four in Canada. At this point no attempt has been made to systematically explore differences between the field in the United States and the field in other countries. An effort was made to include labels from important punk scenes in the USA and Canada: Long Island, New Jersey, Florida, Austin, San Diego, Los Angeles, San Francisco, Portland, Minneapolis and Chicago. The method used is not a rolling sample (in which interviewees suggest the next interviewees) but an attempt to choose representative examples of different types of label. Important labels such as Havoc and Alternative Tentacles were included along with fairly commercial enterprises and some very small labels. There was sometimes an element of chance in who participated. Labels were not chosen from a fan's point of view: a label did not have to be "important" to be included.

At the beginning of the research I was concerned at the difficulty in getting responses from larger and commercial labels. They receive a vast amount of e-mail and it was often difficult to get a reply. Some may have been wary of research on the music industry which might end up by questioning their claim to be an independent label or distributor. DIY labels are usually smaller and more willing to regard participation in the research as solidarity with a member of the scene: and one from Canada. But somewhat to my surprise many larger commercial labels were willing to participate. I would like to interview more record labels in the future, though I was often surprised at the extent of coverage that I achieved. For example, although I did not get to interview Gold Standard Laboratories, I did talk with two similar labels in San Diego. I would have liked to include Six Weeks, but did speak with a good friend of theirs at Tankcrimes, and Sound Pollution is somewhat similar. Certainly I would have liked to interview Fat Wreck Chords, but New Red Archives are friends and the two labels operate in similar ways. Hopeless Records is musically more diverse but otherwise similar to Fat Wreck. I look forward to visiting Seattle but did talk with two people who had previously lived in that city. I was not able to interview Ruth Schwartz but I did talk with three ex-employees and with many labels previously distributed by Mordam.

About eight record labels declined to be interviewed. The reasons were different in each case and I am satisfied that there was no pattern of refusals that would affect the research findings. Most of the interviews were done in person in 2006. Two or three people requested to respond to questions by e-mail. Some people who could not be interviewed in person later took part in telephone interviews. This helped eliminate bias against people with day jobs who are less available for interviews. Many such people were interviewed before or after work or on the weekend. A few people who were missed because of work were later interviewed by telephone. I hope to interview more record labels and in five different countries for a second, expanded edition of this book. Research for the book was entirely self-funded. Thanks to everyone who participated in interviews, responded to e-mails and otherwise helped.

Years operating: counted to the end of 2006

Number of titles: Vinyl and CD versions are counted as one release. Some labels give them separate numbers. When a label was restarted and renamed only the current label's releases are counted.

Normal pressing: The question asked was the most usual first pressing for a release. This figure is therefore estimates of the median rather than the mean. Most labels report a drop in sales after the year 2000. For labels that existed in the 1990s the figure is usually their normal pressing in that period.

Highest sales: This is the total of vinyl, CDs and cassettes for the best-selling recording on the label. Since this is the best selling release in the label's history it usually does not include electronic sales, since these are still quite small for punk labels in 2006.

Review copies: This seems a good measure of how businesslike the label is run. The number is for the usual amount of review copies sent out per release. It is normally for 2006 unless the label has recently changed its policy (some labels are sending out fewer review copies because of the perceived decline in importance of fanzines) in which case the previous number is used. This number does not include free copies supplied to distributors for retailers.

Father's occupation: Mother's occupation is used here when Father is deceased or absent. The research uses the occupational scale from Peterson and Simkus (1992). This scale takes into account changes in the occupational structure, the shift to services and the importance of educational qualifications. It is not a measure of income but of occupational status: income and cultural capital combined. The scale seems close to the intentions of Bourdieu's sociology. Peterson and Simkus give representative examples for each occupational group.

19. Higher Cultural. Architects, lawyers, clergymen, librarians, academics.
18. Lower Cultural. Social workers, teachers below college, religious workers, public relations.
17. Artists. Actors, authors, dancers, editors, musicians, painters.
16. Higher Technical. Chemical engineers, actuaries, chemists, geologists, physicians, dentists.
15. Lower Technical. Accountants, computer programmers, chiropractors, pharmacists, registered nurses, health technicians, dieticians.
14. Higher Managerial. Owners, managers, administrators, officials, superintendents, with income greater than $30,000 in 1981.
13. Lower Managerial. Owners, managers, administrators, officials, superintendents, with incomes less than $30,000 in 1981.
12. Higher Sales. Insurance agents, real estate agents, manufacturing sales, stockbrokers.
11. Lower Sales. Newsboys, retail salesclerks, hucksters, peddlers.
10. Clerical. Bank tellers, file clerks, mail carriers, typists, office machine operators, ticket agents, receptionists, meter readers.
 9. Skilled Manual. Bakers, brickmasons, bulldozer operators, carpenters, machinists, mechanics, printers, painters, plumbers, phone installers.

8. Semi-Skilled Transport. Truck, taxi-drivers, deliverymen, forklift operators, railroad switchmen.
7. Semi-Skilled Manual. Factory operatives, gas station attendants, laundry workers, weavers.
6. Laborers. Craft helpers, warehousemen, fishermen, construction laborers, garbage collectors.
5. Skilled Service. Dental assistants, nursing aides, practical nurses, barbers, cosmeticians, airline hostesses.
4. Protective Service. Policemen, sheriffs, firemen, watchmen, marshals, bridge tenders.
3. Unskilled Service. Janitors, maids, waiters, orderlies, porters, cooks.
2. Farmers. Farm owners and family, farm managers.
1. Farm Laborers. Farm workers, farm foremen, farm service laborers.

Years of school

Finished high school = 12
One year of college = 13
Two-year college degree = 14
College degree almost complete = 15
College Degree = 16
MA or MBA = 18
Ph.D. = 22

Where two people were interviewed at a record label the figures used for occupation and education are averages of both scores. In some cases these people are simply coworkers (at Alternative Tentacles) but others are life partners (Schizophrenic Records).

Table B.1.   Statistical Data on Record Labels Interviewed

Label	Years	Titles	Normal Press	Highest Sales	Review Copies	Father's Occup.	Years of School
La Idea	10	30	1,000	20,000	20	9	12
Potencial Hardcore	20	133	1,000	22,000	100	10	12
El Lokal	15	73	1,000	21,000	100	19	14
Grita o Muere	5	21	1,000	1,500	10	15	14
Lengua Armada	15	40	1,000	17,000	10	13	18
Fuck the Bullshit	2	3	1,000	1,000	10	15	12
Schitzophrenic	13	26	1,000	2,000	5	11	14
Search and Rescue	5	7	3,000	9,000	200	14	16
Sound Pollution	16	97	1,000	16,000	50	10	16
Sin Fronteras	10	31	1,000	2,500	5	15	12
Profane Existence	17	98	2,000	15,000	70	16	14

Label	Years	Titles	Normal Press	Highest Sales	Review Copies	Father's Occup.	Years of School
Havoc	15	70	2,000	25,000	100	9	18
A-F Records	9	42	2,000	70,000	200	14	16
Poor Boy	2	5	1,000	1,000	20	18	13
Level Nine	2	1	1,000	1,000	3	14	18
Friction	5	36	1,000	1,000	50	9	13
Punks Before Profits	7	26	1,000	1,500	8	9	11
Doghouse	18	122	5,000	150,000	500	16	12
Jade Tree	16	122	4,000	100,000	400	12	16
Prison Jazz	3	14	1,000	1,500	350	8	16
Equal Vision	15	137	12,000	500,000	2,000	9	15
Gloom	12	39	1,500	7,000	5	14	13
Rok Lok	7	27	500	1,400	15	9	14
Punk Core	10	46	5,000	50,000	500	7	12
Iron Pier	1	6	500	1,000	50	19	14
Faction Zero	3	7	1,000	1,000	20	14	17
Trustkill	12	88	20,000	250,000	2,000	16	20
Chunksaah	15	29	2,000	25,000	200	14	17
Youngblood	10	26	1,500	3,000	150	19	16
Firestarter	4	10	500	1,600	10	14	15
Rat Town	14	10	500	1,000	50	9	14
No Idea	18	198	1,500	90,000	400	12	12
Fueled By Ramen	11	91	20,000	500,000	500	16	18
Sound Idea	15	25	2,000	5,000	6	14	16
Hardcore Holocaust	11	27	2,000	7,500	30	13	14
Taang	25	180	3,000	75,000	500	13	14
Three One G	11	52	2,000	10,000	300	15	12
BYO	24	108	10,000	225,000	1,000	17	15
Go Kart	12	123	2,000	110,000	300	14	16
Revelation	20	142	4,000	100,000	150	13	15
TKO	10	166	2,000	10,000	200	19	13
Hopeless	13	91	5,000	340,000	1,500	14	16
Ebullition	16	60	3,000	13,000	zero	19	16
SAF	4	14	500	2,000	200	14	15
New Red Archives	19	99	3,000	100,000	750	9	12
Asian Man	10	139	2,000	100,000	1,000	15	16
Subterranean	27	77	3,000	75,000	500	13	14
1 2 3 4 Go	5	23	500	2,500	100	6	13
Alternative Tentacles	27	368	2,000	350,000	300	15	14
Accident Prone	9	23	500	1,000	150	12	14
Feral Ward	8	34	3,000	20,000	10	15	15
Dirtnap	6	50	1,000	20,000	300	7	12
Discourage	2	3	1,200	1,000	10	14	16
Deranged	6	87	3,000	8,000	60	16	15
Lovitt	11	52	3,000	20,000	300	5	16
Deep Six	15	72	1,000	10,000	30	15	14
Recess	16	101	2,000	10,000	400	18	12
Gravity	15	32	1,000	9,000	100	15	14
Wrench in the Gears	2	4	600	1,200	10	15	12
Tankcrimes	6	18	1,000	1,600	30	13	14
Dischord	26	160	5,000	800,000	250	17	12

Table B.2. List of Interviews

Label	Location of Label	Person Interviewed	Date	Father's Occupation	Mother's Occupation	Own Occupation
1. La Idea	Madrid	Iñaki	5 June 04	painter (separated)	parking enforcement	record store part-time and musician
2. Potencial hardcore	Madrid	Pilar	5 June 04	electrical firm employee	home-maker	label employee
3. El Lokal	Barcelona	Miguel	9 June 04	lawyer	primary school teacher	record label and works at concerts
4. Grita o Muere	Barcelona	Alejo	10 June 04	artist (separated)	employee for publisher	record label, distro and musician
5. Lengua Armada	Chicago and San Francisco	Martín Sorrondeguy interviewed in Toronto	26 Aug 05	carpentry business	home-maker	teacher part-time, MRR distribution
6. Fuck the Bullshit	Montreal	Jonah Steve	25 May 06	lawyer insurance	sociology teacher univ. admin	data entry record store partner
7. Schitzophrenic	Hamilton, ON	Craig Leah	3 June 06	bus driver commodity trader	home / prev. nurse small publishing	child counselor video production assistant
8. Search and Rescue	Ann Arbor, MI	Jonathan Woods	14 June 06	manufacturing plant manager	architect	sales and account manager auto parts industry

9. Sound Pollution	Covington, KY	Ken Pollution	24 June 06	deceased	doctor's office secretary	federal government accounts management
10. Sin Fronteras	Minneapolis	Kerry Reynolds	12 July 06	absent	nurse	taxicab owner
11. Profane Existence	Minneapolis	Dan	12 July 06	Bureau of Mines geophysicist	microbiologist, medical company quality control	record label
12. Havoc	Minneapolis	Felix Havoc e-mail interview	July 06	land surveyor	typography layout, desk-top publishing	record label and building restoration
13. A-F Records	Pittsburgh	Jorge Orsovay	25 July 06	managerial, technical translator	home-maker	label manager
14. Poor Boy	Boiling Springs, PA	Johnny Hero	26 July 06	deceased	teacher	various day jobs
15. Level Nine Entertainment	York, PA	Greg Bowman	26 July 06	gas station and grocery owner	teacher and home-maker	architect, Internet jobs, student teacher
16. Friction Records	Grand Rapids, MI	Jeff Vanden Berg	8 Aug 06	truck mechanic	dentist's receptionist	silk-screen business
17. Punks Before Profits	Grand Rapids, MI	Ryan Punxxx	9 Aug 06	factory electrician	nurse	service jobs, pizza
18. Doghouse and Lumberjack Mordam	Toledo, OH	Dirk Hemsath	10 Aug 06	chemical engineer	business entrepreneur	label owner
19. Jade Tree	Wilmington, DE	Darren Walters	11 Aug 06	office paper sales	home-maker	label co-owner
20. Prison Jazz	Scranton, PA	Jeanine Dan	12 Aug 06	factory worker electrician	health education Town Clerk	nurse nurse aide

(*continued*)

Table B.2. (continued)

Label	Location of Label	Person Interviewed	Date	Father's Occupation	Mother's Occupation	Own Occupation
21. Equal Vision	Albany, NY	Steven Reddy	5 Sept 06	welder	printing press operator	label owner
22. Gloom	Albany, NY	Nate Wilson	6 Sept 06	director nonprofit	director arts organization	painting foreman
23. Rok Lok	Long Island, NY	Mike Andriani	7 Sept 06	bus driver, mechanic	nurse	publicity for small record label
24. Punk Core	Long Island, NY	Dave Punkcore	7 Sept 06	installs shutters, blinds	school admin assistant	label owner
25. Iron Pier	Long Island, NY	Dave Vibert	8 Sept 06	religious minister	secretary	student and health-food store job
26. Faction Zero	Clifton, NJ	Chris D'Alessandro	9 Sept 06	absent	Vice-Pres. sales file folder company	State employee, human resources student
27. Thrustkill	Tinton Falls, NJ	Josh Grabelle interviewed at show	10 Sept 06	medical doctor	lawyer	label owner, law school graduate
28. Chunksaah	Asbury Park, NJ	Kate Hiltz	11 Sept 06	oil industry executive	information science professor	band business manager
29. Youngblood	Ephratra, NJ	Sean O'Donnell	12 Sept 06	English professor	English professor	newspaper website employee
30. Firestarter	Baltimore	Mike Riley	13 Sept 06	shipping company executive	horse breeder and trainer	bike courier, print shop employee

#	Label	Location	Name	Date			
31.	Rat Town	Jacksonville Beach, FL	Dan Rattown	16 Sept 06	truck, motorbike mechanic	absent	carpenter
32.	No Idea	Gainesville, FL	Var Thelin	18 Sept 06	equipment salesman	home-maker, then various jobs	label owner
33.	Fueled By Ramen	Tampa, FL	John Janick	19 Sept 06	medical doctor	secretary	label owner
34.	Sound Idea	Brandon, FL	Bob Suren	19 Sept 06	head of personnel large company	home-maker	record store owner and distribution
35.	Hardcore Holocaust	Austin	Jay H	22 Sept 06	floor supervisor psych hospital	high school math teacher	label owner and distribution
36.	Taang!	San Diego	Curtis	28 Sept 06	construction work and contractor	home-maker	label owner and record store
37.	Three One G	San Diego	Alysia Edwards	29 Sept 06	deceased	fashion designer	label co-owner and bartender
38.	BYO Records	Marina Del Rey (LA)	Shawn Stern	3 Oct 06	doctor, screen writer and director	secretary, daycare	label co-owner and musician
39.	Go-Kart	New York and Los Angeles	Greg Ross	3 Oct 06	owns chain of fast food restaurants	clothing company 17 employees	label owner
40.	Revelation	Huntington Beach (LA)	Bob Shedd	4 Oct 06	VP Sales food industry	office work	label A&R
			Shane Pacillo		car salesman	nurse	label publicity, student
41.	TKO	Costa Mesa (LA)	Mark Rainey	4 Oct 06	university professor	highschool teacher, historian	label owner, family business
42.	Hopeless	Van Nuys (LA)	Louis Posen	5 Oct 06	manufacturer of restaurant signs	small business	label owner
43.	Ebullition	Goleta, CA	Kent McClard	6 Oct 06	absent	family law attorney	record distributor, label owner
44.	SAF	Santa Cruz	Matt Driscoll	7 Oct 06	United Way CEO	airline ticket agent	pizza-maker

(continued)

Table B.2. (continued)

Label	Location of Label	Person Interviewed	Date	Father's Occupation	Mother's Occupation	Own Occupation
45. New Red Archives	San Francisco	Nicky Garrett	10 Oct 06	electrician for forklift company	home-maker	label owner and musician
46. Asian Man	Monte Serano, CA	Mike Park	12 Oct 06	hospital microbiology technician	hairdresser, then home-maker	label owner and musician
47. Subterranean	San Francisco	Steve Tupper	13 Oct 06	trade-union business agent	newspaper advertising sales	label owner and distribution previously skilled machinist
48. 1-2-3-4 Go!	Oakland, CA	Stevo	14 Oct 06	construction worker, later absent	mill worker, later own business	distribution manager for small merch company
49. Alternative Tentacles	Emeryville, CA	Dave Adelson Jesse Townley	16 Oct 06	oil industry middle mgt. professional writer	various part-time nurse	label manager label mail-order, musician
50. Accident Prone	Portland, OR	Gary Bahen	17 Oct 06	horticulture industry marketing	home-maker	label owner, silk-screen printer and student
51. Feral Ward	Portland, OR	Yannick	18 Oct 06	pharmacist	stockbroker	label owner, screen-printer, musician
52. Dirtnap	Portland, OR	Ken	18 Oct 06	absent	factory work and service jobs	label and record store owner

53. Discourage	Portland, OR	Abe	19 Oct 06	deceased	teacher	co-owners record store and mail-order distribution
		Paul		divorced	state employee	
54. Deranged	Gibsons, BC	Gord Dufresne phone interview	17 Nov 06	oil industry engineer	lab technician, nurse	corporate human resources services
55. Lovitt	Arlington, VA	Brian Lovitt phone interview	21 Nov 06	deceased	elementary school teacher's assist.	Dischord employee and own label
56. Deep Six	Burbank, CA	Bob Deepsix phone interview	23 Nov 06	aircraft industry quality control	mainly home-maker	electronics engineer
57. Recess	San Pedro, CA	Todd C phone interview	28 Nov 06	high school football coach	home-maker, temp secretary	musician, label owner
58. Gravity	San Diego	Matt Anderson phone interview	28 Nov 06	airline pilot	sales training videos	musician, label owner, printer
59. A Wrench in the Gears	Chicago	Mike Friedberg phone interview	30 Nov 06	social worker	bakery cashier	grocery store employee
60. Tankcrimes	Oakland, CA	Scotty Heath / Karate Interviewed in Buffalo	12 Dec 06	bar and restaurant owner	various jobs (divorced)	silk-screen printer, musician, label owner
61. Dischord	Washington, DC area	Ian MacKaye phone interview	11 Jan 07	Journalist and editor	home-maker and writer	label co-owner and musician

Bibliography

The bibliography is in two parts: the first is general books and articles, and the second is material on specific record labels. Some older issues of punk fanzines are available online at www.operationphoenixrecords.com (8 May 2007).

1. General Books and Articles

Albini, Steve. "The Problem with Music." In *Commodify Your Dissent*, ed Thomas Frank and Matt Weiland, 164–76. New York: Norton, 1997. Reprinted from *The Baffler* no. 5, 1991. Also reprinted in *Maximumrocknroll* no. 133, June 1994, 3 pages. Online at http://www.arancidamoeba.com/mrr (24 February 2007).

Anderson, Mark and Mark Jemkins. *Dance of Days: Two Decades of Punk in the Nation's Capital*. New York: Soft Skull Press, 2001.

Azzerrad, Michael. *Our Band Could Be Your Life: Scenes from the American Indie Underground 1981–1991*. Boston: Little, Brown and Company, 2001.

Belsito, Peter and Bob Davis. *Hardcore California: A History of Punk and New Wave*. Berkeley: Last Gasp, 1983.

Bessman, Jim. *Ramones: An American Band*. New York: St. Martin's Press, 1993.

Bourdieu, Pierre. *The Rules of Art: Genesis and Structure of the Literary Field*. Translated by Susan Emanuel. Stanford: Stanford University Press, 1995.

Bourdieu, Pierre. *Distinction: A Social Critique of the Judgement of Taste*. Translated by Richard Nice. Cambridge: Harvard University Press.

Bourdieu, Pierre et al. *The Weight of the World: Social Suffering in Contemporary Society*. Translated by Priscilla Parkhurst Ferguson et al. Stanford: Stanford University Press, 1999.

Carducci, Joe. *Rock and the Pop Narcotic*. Chicago: Redoubt Press, 1990. Part of this is reprinted in *The Penguin Book of Rock and Roll Writing*, ed. Clinton Heylin, 124–50. London: Viking, 1992.

Clausen, Sten-Erik. *Applied Correspondence Analysis: An Introduction*. Thousand Oaks: SAGE, 1998.

Diehl, Matt. *My So-Called Punk*. New York: St. Martin's, 2007.

Gaertner, Joachim. *They Could Have Been Bigger Than EMI: A Discography of Now Defunct Independent Record Labels That Released Vinyl*. Frankfurt, Germany: Pure Pop For New People, 2005.

Glasper, Ian. *Burning Britain: The History of UK Punk 1980–1984*. London: Cherry Red, 2004.

Glasper, Ian. *The Day the Country Died: A History of Anarcho Punk 1980–1984*. London: Cherry Red, 2006.

Greenwald, Andy. *Nothing Feels Good: Punk Rock, Teenagers and Emo*. New York: St. Martin's Press, 2003.

Heartattack no. 20, November 1998. Special issue on DIY. Online at www.operationphoenixrecords.com (8 May 2007).

Henwood, Doug. *After the New Economy*. New York: The New Press, 2005.

Hesmondhalgh, David. "Post-Punk's Attempt to Democratise the Music Industry: the Success and Failure of Rough Trade." *Popular Music* 16, no. 3 (1998): 255–74.

Hull, Geoffrey P. *The Recording Industry*, 2d ed. New York and London: Routledge. 2004.

Hurchalla, George. *Going Underground: American Punk 1979–1992*. Stuart FL: Zuo Press, 2006.

Hustwit, Gary. *Releasing an Independent Record*, 4th ed. San Diego: Rockpress, 1993.

Jaerich, Burkhard. *Flex! U.S. Hardcore Discography*. 2d ed. Germany: Flex!, 2001.

Kovach, W. L. *MVSP—A MultiVariate Statistical Package for Windows*. Ver. 3.1. Pentraeth, Wales: Kovach Computing Services, 2005.

Maximumrocknroll no. 104, January 1992. Special issue on Punk Business.

Maximumrocknroll no. 133, June 1994. Special issue on Major Labels. Online at www.arancidamoeba.com/mrr (24 February 2007).

Maximumrocknroll no. 276 and 277, May and June 2006. Special issues on Business and Punk Rock.

Mudrian, Albert. *Choosing Death: the Improbable History of Death Metal and Grindcore*. Los Angeles: Feral House, 2004.

Myers, Ben. *Green Day: American Idiots & The New Punk Explosion*. New York: Disinformation, 2006.

Peterson, Richard A. and Albert Sumkus. "How Musical Tastes Mark Occupational Status Groups." In *Cultivating Differences: Symbolic Boundaries and the Making of Inequality*, ed. Michele Lamont and Marcel Fournier, 153–86. Chicago and London: University of Chicago, 1992.

Reynolds, Simon. *Rip It Up and Start Again: Post-Punk 1978–84*. London: Faber and Faber, 2005.

Sakolsky, Ron and Fred Wei-Han Ho, eds. *Sounding Off! Music as Subversion / Resistance / Revolution.* New York: Autonomedia, 1995.

Simple Machines. *The Mechanic's Guide.* Raleigh NC: Barefoot Press, 1991. Available online at www.indiecenter.com (15 July 2006).

Sinker, Daniel ed. *We Owe You Nothing: Punk Planet: The Collected Interviews.* New York: Akashic Books, 2001.

Sprouse, Martin, ed. *Threat By Example.* San Francisco: Pressure Drop Press, 1990.

Young, Rob. *Rough Trade.* London: Black Dog Publishing, 2006.

2. Articles on Specific Record Labels and Distributors

Arenas, Norm. "Ian Mackaye: Dischord Founder Speaks on Becoming Your Own Boss." *Anti-Matter* no. 4, Spring 1994, 14–19.

Arnold, Gina. *Kiss This: Punk in the Present Tense.* New York: St. Martin's, 1997. Chapter 9 on Epitaph.

August, Ryan. "Prank Records: An Interview with Prank Records' Ken Sanderson." *AMP*, January 2003. Online at www.ampmagazine.com (24 February 2007).

Bertsch, Charlie. "Matador Records." *Punk Planet* no. 36, March-April 2000, 30–35.

Brian G.T.A. "How To Start A Record label." Column in *Maximumrocknroll* no. 178, March 1998, 3 pages. Includes details about Grand Theft Audio.

Cantu, Bob. "Sub Pop." Interview in *Flipside* no. 85, July–August 1993, 2 pages.

Carriere, Michael. "Cory Rusk: Touch & Go Records." *Punk Planet* no. 76, November–December 2006, 26–31.

Catucci, Nick. "Jade Tree's World of Difference." *Boston Phoenix*, 17 January 2000.

Dan. "Skuld Releases." *Profane Existence* no. 50–51, 47–69. Interview and illustrated discography.

Downhill Battle. "Ian Mackaye: Fugazi / Dischord." 20 January 2004. Online at www.downhillbattle.org (29 June 2006).

Fritch, Matthew. "Frontier Days: Homestead Records." *Magnet* no. 72, July–August 2006, 76–83.

Generic. "Pioneers of Punk: Dangerhouse." *Maximumrocknroll* no. 179, April 1998, 4 pages.

Harvilla, Rob. "Kerplunk: The Rise and Fall of the Lookout Records Empire." *East Bay Express*, 14 September 2005. Online at www.eastbayexpress.com (24 February 2007).

Havoc, Felix. Column about Havoc Records. *Maximumrocknroll* no. 277, June 2006, 2 pages.

Hopper, Jessica. "Slowdime Records." *Punk Planet* no. 21, November–December 1997, 52–53.

IndieHQ. "Lumberjack Mordam Music Group 1 Year Later." 20 April 2006. Online at http://indiehq.com (15 August 2006).

Lahickey, Beth. "Jordan Cooper." In *All Ages: Reflections on Straightedge*, ed. Beth Lahickey, 51–58. Huntington Beach, CA: Revelation Books, 1997. Interview with Revelation Records.

Lee, Jonathan. "Council Records." *Heartattack* no. 31, August 2001, 2 pages. Interview with Matt Weeks.

Livermore, Larry. "Lookout Records: The Story So Far, or How I Became a Capitalist," *Lookout* no. 39, Summer 1994, 33–37, 46.

Mason, Jeff. "Crimes Against Humanity Records." *Maximumrocknroll* no. 283, December 2006, 4 pages.

Mayo, Rama. "Lumberjack Distribution: The Big Takeover." *Punk Planet* no. 20, September–October 1997, 49–53.

MRR. "Ax/ction Records." *Maximumrocknroll* no. 46, March 1987, 1 page.

MRR. Documents relating to Screeching Weasel and Lookout Records. *Maximumrocknroll* no. 168, May 1997, 5 pages.

MRR. Interview with Chris Spedding and Other People's Music. *Maximumrocknroll* no. 165, February 1997, 2 pages.

MRR. "En Guard Records." *Maximumrocknroll* no. 140, January 1995, 1 page.

Mundo. "Chapter Eleven: Interview with Ian and Saul of Chapter 11 Records and the Randumbs." *Maximumrocknroll* no. 179, April 1998, 3 pages.

Paris, Amy. "Bring the Noise: Will the Exodus of Distributors and Indie Labels from Overpriced SF turn Sacramento into More of a Musical Hotspot." *Sacramento News and Review*, 8 March 2001, News and Features. Online at www.newsreview.com (19 February 2007).

Perry, Stephe. "Lengua Armada Records." *Maximumrocknroll* no. 225, February 2002, 5 pages.

Perry, Stephe. "Six Two Five." *Maximumrocknroll* no. 237, February 2003, 5 pages.

Pierson, John R, Jughead and Ian Pierce. *Weasels in a Box*. Chicago: Hope & Nonthings, 2005, 227–33. Fictional account of Lookout! Records and Fat Wreck Chords.

Punk News. "Vinnie Talks about his Departure from Fueled By Ramen." Punknews.org, 23 December 2006. Online at www.punknews.org (23 December 2006).

Punk Planet. "Lovitt Records." *Punk Planet* no. 23, March–April 1998, 58–61.

Profane Existence. "Active Distribution." *Profane Existence* no. 23, Autumn 1994, 8–9.

Profane Existence. "Epitaph versus Boycot." *Profane Existence* no. 35, April–June 1998, 56–58. Discussion between two members of the band Boycot and two European employees of Epitaph Records.

Profane Existence. Announcement of suspension of activities. *Heartattack* no. 20, November 1998, 1 page.

Rutledge, Josh. "Patrick Grindstaff of Pelado Records." *Maximumrocknroll* no. 171, August 1997, 2 pages.

Rutledge, Josh. "They Still Make Records." *Maximumrocknroll* no. 179, April 1998, 2 pages.

Ryan, Kyle. "Tony Brummel." *The Onion,* 1–7 December 2005, 30. Interview with Victory Records.

Ryan, Kyle. "Mega Merger in the Indie World: After Two Decades in Business Mordam Records Accepts a Buyout from Competitor Lumberjack Distribution." *Punk Planet* no. 66. Online at www.emykyle.com (19 February 2007).

Scanner. "Recess Interview." *Scanner* no. 12 [England]. Online at www.recessrecords.com (20 November 2006).

Schalit, Joel. "Subterranean Distribution." *Punk Planet* no. 23, March–April 1998, 50–53.

Schoemer, Karen. "Punk Is His Business: How Epitaph Records became the hottest little label in the industry." *Newsweek,* 30 January 1995, 58–59.

Sean S. "Label Spotlight: Hopscotch Records." *Maximumrocknroll* no. 196, September 1999, 4 pages.

Sinker, Daniel. Interview with G7 Welcoming Committee Records. *Punk Planet* no. 89, July–August 2007, 24–27.

Tabb, George. Column about Larry Livermore and Lookout Records. *Maximumrocknroll* no. 165, February 1997, 5 pages.

TooCrass, Jeb. "This Ain't Oprah: Interview with Chris Dodge of Slap A Ham Records." *Crass Menagerie* no. 100, part five, 2003. Online at www.geocities.com/toocrass (24 February 2007).

Tung, Chi. "Peace, Unity and Ska-Punk Music: Interview with Mike Park." *Asia Pacific Arts,* 9 January, 2004. Online at www.asiaarts.ucla.edu (28 July 2006).

Yohannan, Tim. "Dangerhouse Records." *Maximumrocknroll* no. 99, August 1991. Online at www.breakmyface.com (28 June 2006).

Ziegler, Chris. "Plan-It-X Records." *Punk Planet* no. 44, July–August 2001, 46–48.

Index

Faction Zero, 50, 53
Factory Records, 19
Faith No More, 44n6
Fancher, Lisa, 11n12
fanzines. *See* zines
Fat Wreck Chords, x, 74, 78, 80
Faulty Products, 3, 19, 29n4, 35, 36
feminism, 56
Feral Ward, 51, 70, 75
field, 3–4, 9, 15, 16, 87; boundaries of,
    73, 76–77; in Britain, 19; in Canada,
    19; contemporary, 59–61, 62–63,
    67–82, 87–88; dual structure of,
    24–28; expansion of in 1990s, 71–73
Filth, 96
Fiorello, Vinnie, 22
Firestarter Records, 54, 74
The Fix, 82
Flaubert, Gustave, 4, 16
Flipper, 50, 67
Flipside, 7, 12n17
Fontana, x
Franklin, 70
Frente Sandinista de Liberación
    Nacional (FSLN), 97
Fresh Fruit for Rotting Vegetables, 3, 10n8
Friction Records, 60
Fringe Product, 19
Frontier Records, 9
Fuck the Bullshit Records, 52, 60
Fueled By Ramen, 22, 59
Fuerza X, 103
Fugazi, 11n14, 13, 68, 81, 99
F.Y.P. (band), 72

Garratt, Nicky, 2. *See also* New Red
    Archives
Get Up Kids, 78
Gilman Street, 24, 67
Gloom Records, 9, 69, 70
gold record, x
Gold Standard Laboratories, 25

Gossett, Richard, 49
Government Issue, 21
Grabelle, Josh, 59. *See also* Trustkill
    Records
Gravity Records, 28, 69, 83n6
Great American Steak Religion, 70
Green Day, 22, 24, 31n19, 39, 41, 72,
    76
Grita o Muere, 60
Groff, Skip, 6
guarantees, band, 30n14
Gurewitz, Bret, 31n18

habitus, 47, 59, 86, 88
Hardcore Holocaust, 42
Havoc, Felix, 61. *See also* Havoc Records
Havoc Records, ix, 9, 60, 69, 77, 100
Haynes, Patrick, 40
Heartattack zine, 12n18, 39, 48, 111
Heavy Metal. *See* Metal
Hemsath, Dirk, 22, 33n23, 40–41, 64,
    78. *See also* Doghouse; Lumberjack
Hiltz, Jon, 32n21, 53–54
Hiltz, Kate, 32n21, 40, 53–54. *See also*
    Chunksaah Records
Histeria compilations, 102–3
Hit List zine, 38
Homestead Records, 30n12
homophobia, 56, 91n6, 98
Hopeless Records, 28, 59, 69, 78, 83n5
Hot Topic, 51
Hüsker Dü, 21

I Object!, 75
I Quit!, 103
Internet sales, 40, 79. *See also* digital
    downloads
interpersonal communication, 51
Interpunk.com, 42
Iron Pier Records, 53
I.R.S. Records, 3, 17, 35
iTunes, 81, 82

About the Author

Alan O'Connor is author of *The Voice of the Mountains: Radio and Anthropology* (University Press of America, 2006), *Raymond Williams* (Rowman and Littlefield, 2005), and editor and translator of *Community Radio in Bolivia: The Miner's Radio Stations* (Edwin Mellen, 2004). One of the founders of the infoshop Who's Emma in Toronto in the 1990s, he has also written a series of articles on punk scenes in Mexico, the United States, Canada, and Spain. He teaches in the Cultural Studies Program at Trent University in Canada.